AF449199

Globalization, Liberalization and Economic Development

Globalization, Liberalization and Economic Development

By

Basudeb Sahoo

Director, Jayaprakash Narayan Institute of
Economics and Social Studies,
Bhubaneswar, Odisha.

New Century Publications
New Delhi, India

NEW CENTURY PUBLICATIONS
4800/24, Bharat Ram Road,
Ansari Road, Daryaganj,
New Delhi – 110 002 (India)

Tel.: 011-2324 7798, 4358 7398, 6539 6605
Fax: 011-4101 7798
E-mail: indiatax@vsnl.com • info@newcenturypublications.com
www.newcenturypublications.com

Editorial office:
LG–7, Aakarshan Bhawan,
4754-57/23, Ansari Road, Daryaganj,
New Delhi – 110 002

Tel.: 011-4356 0919

First Published: **July 2013**

ISBN: **978-81-7708-349-1**

Published by New Century Publications and printed at Salasar Imaging Systems, New Delhi.

Designs: Patch Creative Unit, New Delhi.

PRINTED IN INDIA

To My Loving Students

About the Book

Globalization is widely seen as the most important factor that could influence economies of nations the world over in the new millennium. A major feature of globalization is the growing concentration and monopolisation of economic resources and power by transnational corporations and by global financial firms and funds. This process has been termed transnationalization, in which fewer and fewer transnational corporations are gaining a large and rapidly increasing proportion of world's economic resources, production and market share.

Economic liberalization in India started in the early 1990s, and encompassed wide-ranging reform measures in the areas of industry, public finance, banking and insurance, foreign trade and exchange rate management. Economic reforms, though slowed down lately, are aimed at reorientation of the centrally controlled economy to a market-oriented one in order to foster greater efficiency and growth.

India's recent economic performance has, indeed, been creditable. However, such growth must make a demonstrable difference to the lives of the poorest and most vulnerable citizens. India has the potential and the means to secure a reasonable standard of living for all of its citizens. Inclusive growth necessarily implies concerted efforts, by all levels of government, to invest in the delivery of public services, particularly those which promote progress in social sectors like health and education.

This book deals with India's recent development experience in the context of globalization, focusing on the need for inclusive growth.

Author's Profile

Dr. Basudeb Sahoo is presently Director, Jayaprakash Narayan Institute of Economics and Social Studies, Bhubaneswar, Odisha. He retired as Professor of Economics, Ravenshaw College, Utkal University. He was also Senior Fellow at Gokhale Institute of Politics and Economics, Pune.

Dr. Sahoo obtained his Ph.D. degree from Utkal University in 1994. He has published numerous books and research papers in referred national and international journals of repute. His areas of specialization include development economics, rural development and monetary policy. He is also the editor of the journal *Vision*.

Contents

Preface

There is undoubtedly much greater economic integration among the nations of the world today. Globalization is widely seen as the most important factor that could influence economies of nations the world over in the new millennium. The rapid advancement in information technology and communications has made it not just possible but absolutely essential for economies of the world to adapt or fall by the wayside.

A major feature of globalization is the growing concentration and monopolisation of economic resources and power by transnational corporations and by global financial firms and funds. This process has been termed transnationalization, in which fewer and fewer transnational corporations are gaining a large and rapidly increasing proportion of world economic resources, production and market shares. Where a multinational company used to dominate the market of a single product, a big transnational company (TNC) now typically produces or trades in an increasing multitude of products, services and sectors. Through mergers and acquisitions, fewer and fewer of these TNCs now control a larger and larger share of the global market, whether in commodities, manufactures or services.

Another feature of the current globalization process is the globalization of national policies and policy-making mechanism. National policies (including economic, social, cultural and technological) that until recently were determined by the States and people within a country have increasingly come under the influence of international agencies and processes or by big private corporations and economic/financial players. This has led to the narrowed ability of governments and people to make choices from options in economic, social and cultural policies.

In India, the liberalization process, which started in the early 1990s, encompassed wide-ranging reform measures in the areas of industry, public finance, banking and insurance, foreign trade and exchange rate management. The purpose of these economic reforms was two-fold: (a) to restore macroeconomic stability on both domestic and external fronts, and (b) to place the economy on a higher growth path through enhanced levels of investment, and improvements in productivity, efficiency and competitiveness.

Economic reforms, though slowed down lately, are aimed at reorientation of the centrally controlled economy to a market-oriented one in order to foster greater efficiency and growth. This is being done by introducing greater competition in the economy through progressive internal deregulation accompanied by external competition promoted by foreign direct investment and trade liberalisation. No area of the Indian economy has been as much influenced by the impulses of reforms as the industrial sector.

To ensure that benefits of development planning flow to all parts of the country, regional balanced development has all along been accepted as an important national objective. However, the pattern of economic reforms over the years has not promoted this cherished objective. It has left in its trail a variety of inequalities which have caused socio-politico tensions. Some States (Karnataka, Andhra Pradesh, Maharashtra) have surged ahead while others are lagging behind. While the economy has performed well, since mid-1980s, in terms of growth rate of GDP, its performance in terms of human development indicators has been unsatisfactory.

Economic reforms of the last 20 years have not paid adequate attention to the social sector (health, education etc.). There is a feeling in some quarters that the industrial growth of India is becoming elite-oriented by registering relatively large increase in the production of electronics items, beverages, cosmetics, motor cars, refrigerators, and finer variety of textiles. It needs to be emphasised that 70 percent of India's population still lives in rural areas.

Inclusive growth is the cornerstone of India's development efforts. India's recent economic growth performance has, indeed, been creditable. However, such growth must make a demonstrable difference to the lives of the poorest and most vulnerable citizens. India has the potential and the means to secure a reasonable standard of living for all of its citizens. Inclusive growth necessarily implies concerted effort, by all levels of government, to invest in the delivery of public services, particularly those which promote progress in social sectors like health and education. However, to achieve this potential, it is necessary that resources are mobilised and deployed in such a manner that the benefits of high rates of growth percolate to ordinary people, particularly those living below poverty line.

I place on record my deep sense of gratitude to my publisher New Century Publications, New Delhi for co-operating with me at various stages of the finalization of this work.

Bhubaneswar
May, 2013

Basudeb Sahoo

1

Economic Development in the Context of Social Change

"The World turns and the time changes.
But one thing does not change,
The perpetual struggle of good and evil".
T.S. Eliot

Man as an individual and a member of the society goes on striving at any stage of evolution of civilization for the good and confronts the forces of evil. The concept of 'good' or for that matter any term like 'development' changes with time with the growth of man's idea and thinking. 'Development' is an oft spoken term conveying diverse meaning, narrow and broad. In narrower sense, it refers to economic development, but in a broader sense, it covers all faces of human life, social, cultural, educational, and moral in addition to economic or material. Thus, the term 'national development' encompasses socio-cultural-political and economic development. Development is taken to mean growth plus change–change in process of production, institution and attitudes and values. Economic development, as Myrdal points out, may be defined "as nothing less than the upward movement of the entire social system". [1]

It is interpreted as the attainment of number of ideals of modernization 'such as rise in productivity, social and economic equalization, modern knowledge, improved institutions, attitudes and a rationally coordinated system of policy measures that can remove undesirable conditions in social system that have perpetuated a state of underdevelopment. [2]

The concept of economic development has itself

undergone change. It no longer consists of aggregate growth of income—it has very much emphasized redistribution. Mehboob Huk in late 1960s raised the question and Hollis Chenery in his introduction to the World Bank's study "Redistribution with Growth" observed, "It is now clear that more than a decade of rapid growth in under developed countries has been of little benefit to perhaps a third of their population though average per capita income had grown by 50 percent in the development decade of 1960s". [3]

Understanding development, nay economic development, has led to bringing out a distinction between economic development and economic growth. "Economic development is a process whereby an economy's real national income increases over a long period of time". [4]

Economic development is a process whereas economic growth is a result thereof. The components of growth are increase in population and saving. Schumpeter characterizes economic development as discontinuous technological change. As to the distinction between economic development and economic growth, it will suffice to state that economic development is a process of growth and economic progress is synonymous with economic welfare. The concept of welfare brings in the significance of the distribution of real national income.

Our understanding of development has undergone evolutionary charges.

1. First, development is not confined to simply economic development. The term has enveloped both economic and non-economic aspects.
2. Of course, economic element is predominant in development of a country—the concept of economic development has also changed over time. In the initial stage of study of development economics, development referred to aggregate real national income. But later on, the idea of people's welfare led to seeing economic development both in aggregate and disaggregates forms.

Along with total real income, average per capita income and particularly percolation of the total growth to the poorer sections of the people, i.e. more equitable distribution of income and welfare became an integral part of development.

3. With the expansion of the attraction of the social welfare ideas, the components of people's welfare has also changed or broadened. Along with the per capita real income, other matters like education, health, longevity etc. have been taken into consideration to measure the level of development.

This has resulted in emergence of human development concept. The HDR, 1995 stated, "The concept of human development is much broader than the conventional theories of economic development. Economic growth models deal with expanding GNP rather than enhancing the quality of human lives. Human development brings together the production and distribution of commodities and the expansion and use of human capabilities. There are four major elements in the concept of human development, viz. productivity, equity, sustainability and empowerment. The profile of human development includes, life expectancy, population with access to health services, access to safe water, access to sanitation, daily calorie supply as percentage of requirements, adult literacy rate, combined primary and secondary enrolment ratio, GNP per capita and real GDP per capita. Since 1990s, the UNDP has brought out this concept and on the basis of the above brought out a composite index to rank the countries of the world on this basis.

Three indicators are there: (i) life expectancy, (ii) educational attainment, and (iii) GDP per capita for decent life. Another idea regarding development that has emerged is sustainable development which means "development that meets the needs of the present without compromising the ability of future generations to meet their own needs" (Hallem Brandt). Sustainable development means much more than maintaining intact the physical capital that produces an income stream in line with population growth. It means maintainable replacement and growth of capital assets both physical and human.

Not only physical but also human capital, even cultural capital has to be maintained, inventiveness to substitute for exhaustible resources hold out for sustainability.

It involves maintaining the physical environment conditions—the constituents of well being. It implies avoiding polluting the water, air, land and exhaustion of renewable resources that are essential for production unless adequate replacement is provided.

Another aspect of sustainability is resilience—system is able to adjust to shocks and crises and be flexible and diverse; avoiding burdening future generations with internal and external debt. Fiscal administrative and political sustainability be aimed at; policies must be credible and acceptable to people (Paul Streeten, What do we owe to the future?, Resource Policy, March, 1986). 80 percent of population on developing countries account for 20 percent of world consumption. 40 percent population in these countries is 15 years old.

Hence, our responsibility is towards future generations. Further, development has been understood in terms of social welfare. Right from the time of A.C. Pigou's 'Wealth and Welfare' (1912), social welfare has drawn the attention of the economists. In 1939, J.R. Hicks, "The Foundation of Welfare Economics" and later Arrow's, "Social Choice and Individual Values" (1951), Sen's, "Collective Choice and Social Welfare" and Rawl's, "Study of Social Justice" and finally Nobel prize was awarded to Arrow and Sen created lively interest in the welfare aspect of development. Sen traversing from the axiomatic theory of social choice to empirical study of poverty, famine has highlighted how social welfare is maximized by creating capacities of individuals based on health and education and the responsibility of the state to strive for equality and greater democratization of society which promote well-being. Welfare has been linked up with ethics. Sen challenged the assumption of self-interest minimization as the best appropriation to actual human behaviour; self-interest behaviours replaced by rule based behaviour like duty, loyalty and good-will achieve individual and groups' efficiency (Ethics and Economics).

Development is a multi-coloured phenomenon painted by various forces, socio-economic, political and cultural. Of these, economic force is the most powerful one which influences the other and is influenced by them. The interrelationship between various forces makes the study of development difficult but interesting. The nature and shape of development change with the change of social setup, which is moulded by ideas on religion, politics, production and distribution. In short, social change brings about a change in the form of development, particularly economic development. "Social change is reflected in changes in production methods, class relation, institution and political system governing a nation".

The social consciousness generated by the socio-economic relations gives rise to appropriate economic system. Marx pointed out that in the social production of their existence men inevitably enter into definite relations of production appropriate to a given stage in the development of their material forces of production. The totality of those relations of production constitutes the economic structure of the society, the real foundation on which results in a legal and political superstructure and to which corresponds a definite form of social consciousness. [5] The complex social influences have impact on individual tastes and changes Dr. Graff admits, "Little room is left for doubt about the extent to which tastes are moulded by social forces". [6]

Society changes with time with new ideas and it gives rise to new economic system. The system springs from certain base made up of tradition, heritage and people's attitude. As Mrs. Robinson observed, "any economic system, requires a set of rules, an ideology to justify them and a conscience in the individual which makes him strive to carry them out." [7]

The idea of development develops in relation to the economic system operating in a nation. Concrete nature of a nations economy is determined by five sets of moulding forces: (a) historic cultural sources of its people's ideals desires, and attitude, (b) its natural resources including climate, (c) philosophers and (d) past and present theorizing of its people about how to achieve chosen ideals and goals, trials and errors of people in seeking economic end". [8] Economic system is built upon three bases such as: (i) technological basis, (ii) institutional basis, machineries through which economic system is run and (iii) ideological base, set of belief opinions and doctrine about social, economic and political phenomena.

Social Change

Society can be looked upon as a process, as a series of interactions between human beings, each person stimulating another person and responding to the stimulation from the other person. Society has developed in an evolutionary process through the interactions of the individuals among themselves and response of the individuals to the challenges of the environment.

Social change is defined as the process which is discernible to significant alteration in the structure and functioning of a particular social system. Social change means change in social behaviours, social structure and social and cultural values.

Social change, says Maclver, occurs in a wave like manner, Max Weber speaks of close relationship between historical, sociological causality—protestant ethic giving rise to spirit of capitalism. August Come (18th century) thinks, social change is the outcome of intellectual development, the logical mood to present science, moral development, from egoism and to altruision bringing about change in social institution. To Marx, social development is caused not by new idea of truth or justice but by the change in productive forces. As productive forces change, they come into conflict with the existing relations of production—worker and masters—inherent contradiction develops.

This engenders social revolution. Marx and Engels say, "Increased needs produce new social relations and increased human produce new needs" (Collective work, Vol. 3 p. 29). Social movements is a process of natural history governed by laws that are not only independent of men's will, consciousness and intentions but on the contrary determine their will, consciousness and intentions'. Society, according to Marx comprised moving balance of antithetical forces that cause social change by the tension and struggle.;For him, struggle rather than peaceful growth was the engine of progress, strife was the faith of all things, and social conflict the core of historical processing.

Marx depicted four stages through which society has moved. These four stages consist of primitive communism, slavery, feudalism and capitalism. The innate contradiction of capitalism will install socialism in which "from each according to his ability, to each according to his needs shall be ascribed.

Institutions

Each state of social revolution has been represented by an appropriate institution, through which the dominant class exercises power over the rest of the society. A society initially guided by a set of institutions gets 'locked in' an inefficient set of institutions because of the interest of the power holder in their reproduction. [9] North (1990) says, the increasing returns characteristics of an initial set up of institutions that proved disincentive to productive activity will create organizations and interest groups with a stake in the existing constraints.

They will shape policy in their interest". [10] North also speaks of a dynamic model of economic change as an integral part of that model analysis of the polity. Harris refers to the, relative backwardness of Hindi heartland and attributes to its hierarchical social set up which got shattered by powerful political mobilization of south and west of India. Similarly, the family firms in India heavily depending on personalized kinship network is a disadvantage in the context of globalization regarding investment due to non-presence of transparency. The family trust of family business is breaking down because of loosening of relationship. The shift from selective trust to abstract principle of business trust is causing problem for India's investment. [11] There is a lot of truth in what David said, "If we learn anything from the history of economic development, it is that culture makes all the difference". [12]

Long back Aristotle pointed out social transformation is based on four factors: (i) political system, (ii) sense of justice, (iii) leadership, and (iv) proper laws and regulations. Karl Marx pointed out that when an idea possesses the minds of the common mass, it becomes a powerful instrument of social transformation.

Thus, when in the world ideas are changing, political system wielding influence is changing and in many countries production method-relation, caste and class relation and above all cultural and moral ethos are changing. With understanding of development, efforts are bound to change and with the acceptance of the changed idea of development efforts be made for the desired goal.

Our understanding of social change is meaningful for appropriate measure to achieve maximum possible welfare or well being for all people. The understanding of the goal of development and constituents or dimensions of welfare has also been changed and broadened. This understanding suggests and urges for effective measures for realization of the desired goal. The changes taking place in recent years engulf the entire world and the states therein. Not-withstanding specific distinct culture and traditions of each state, there are certain changes, which influence at times the entire world. In recent years, some such changes have taken place, which it would be unwise not to bear in mind. The changes moulding almost all societies in the world comprise:

1. Decline of the hold of communism with the collapse of the Soviet block.
2. Rising wave of market economy, free and liberal.
3. Loosening of the state hold on various aspects of human life.
4. Spread of the idea of democratic decentralization and growing role of the non-government voluntary organizations.
5. Greater integration of the countries of the world. Rapid move of cultural and ideological impact from one part of the world to the others.
6. Change in the concept of development, its measure and approach.
7. Seething problems of transition from interventionist society to liberal one, conflict of religious fundamentalism and catholicity. Discontent of the countries at the arbitrary and imposing action of super power like US in the unipolar world.

Countries are to plan their future development programme keeping in mind the change that has taken place. The World Development Report, 1997 rightly stated.

"History and recent experiences have also taught us that development is not just about getting the right economic and technical inputs. It is also about the underlying institutional environment, the rules and customs that determine how these inputs are used". [13]

The most important of all is to know the changed rule of the state. Two vital aspects of the change are:

1. The focus of the State's activities is to be to match its ability. Many states try too much with few resources and little capability. This is to be stopped.
2. Overtime, the state has to look for ways to improve the states capability by reinvigorating public institutions

through designing effective rules and restraints, checking arbitrary state actions and combating entrenched corruption, increasing competitiveness and efficiency.

Global economic and social forces have changed prevailing notions of the state; however it retains the distinctive role in providing public goods that promote economic and social development. The state has to address externalities, basic education, environmental protection regulating monopoly, utility, overcoming imperfect information, insurance, financial regulation, providing social infrastructure and redistribution of assets.

The State has to refocus on its effectiveness. Napoleon I wrote, 'men are powerless to secure the future, institutions alone fix the destinies of nations" (1815). The state can improve development outcomes: (i) by providing a macro economic and a micro economic environment that sets the right incentives for economic activity, (ii) by providing the institutional infrastructure, property rights, law, order and rules that encourage long-term investment, (iii) by fostering market through liberalization of appropriate industrial policy and (iv) by ensuring provision of basic education, health etc. and the physical infrastructure required for economic activity.

Attempt has to be made to bring the state closer to people through electoral participation, improving institutional capability. A Survey in 1991-92 revealed that 49 percent of respondents of UK, 44 percent of USA felt excluded from public decision-making that directly affect their lives. Yet in Western Europe 54 percent and in North America 64 percent of respondents were satisfied with the way democracy is working.

However, in Latin America and Eastern Europe, the satisfied respondents were 30 percent and 40 percent respectively. In EU countries, a 1996 survey revealed that 51 percent believed their government to maintain present social benefits protection level; in Latin America, 69 percent of citizens believe that state should intervene to reduce income difference between the rich and the poor. A 1996 survey shows decline of people's trust in democracy, since 1971. In 1996, trust in police was only 28 percent and in bureaucracy 37 percent, in India. 80 percent respondents in USA mistrusted their government because of perceived inefficiency and waste.

Along with the expansion of people's organization, non-government organizations are to be encouraged to come up with dedication to help people advance in economic, educational and social fields. In 1980s, NGOs covered about 100 million people in developing countries. Now they cover about 250 million people. The Gramya Bank in Bangladesh, Sarvoday Shramdan movement in Sri Lanka, Self-Employed Women's Association in India have marvellous achievements to their credit. Greater people's participation has become imperative.

Increasing opportunities for voice and participation can improve state's capability in three ways: (i) when citizens express their opinions, state acquire some credibility that they need to govern well. Broad based discussion reduces the risk of monopolizing government by powerful minority; (ii) where markets are absent as in public goods, popular voice can reduce information problem and lower transaction costs; (iii) No matter how dedicated and hardworking the officials are, they cannot anticipate all the public goods and services that citizens desire. [14]

Thus, the changed social condition has brought various organizations, at the interface of each other. Now the state, markets, civil society and NGOs interface or intercept each other. They touch and influence each other and have to work in unison if they are to work effectively. Free market economy no doubt reinvigorates the capitalist forces, but at the same time integrates the countries of the world and calls for closer democratic cooperation, coordination of organizations working with and for the people at national and international level.

The changing atmosphere has thrown a new challenge to the states and people to adjust.

"The innovator makes enemies of all those who prospered under the old order and only lukewarm support is forthcoming from those who would prosper under the new" (Nicholas Machiavelli, The Prince, 1513).

There is also a challenge to the working class. They demand higher wages together with high level of investment in schools, roads and machine. Labour-based market demanding growth tends to reduce inequality. Economic growth holds the key. Policies of the state are to be oriented to facilitate long run benefit of the workers who have to cooperate, not resist with much thought with the state. The fate of the 2.5 billion workers in the world is linked with the understanding of the changes and mending their behaviour accordingly.

End Notes

1. Myrdal, G., Asian Drama: An Enquiry into the Poverty of Nations, New York, Random House, 1908, p. 1869.
2. C.E. Black, The Dynamics of Modernization 1966, pp. 55-60.
3. Hollis Chenery et al., Redistribution with Growth, London Oxford University Press, 1974 PXII.
4. J.A. Schumpeter, Theory of Economic Development,pp. 65-66.
5. Karl Marx, A Contribution to the Critique of Political Economy, Progress Publishers, Moscow 1970, p. 20.
6. J. Dev Graff, Theoretical Welfare Economics, Cambridge, 1957, p. 44.
7. Joan Robinson, Economic Philosophy, p. 13.
8. Louck and Whitney, Comparative Economic System, p. 4.
9. Lewis A Closer, Masters of Sociological Thought, HBJ, 1977.
10. North Douglas, Institutions Institutional Change and Economic Performance, Cambridge, University Press.
11. John Harris, Borderlands of Economics-Institutions, Politics and Culture in the Explanation of Economic Change, Indian Journal of Labour Economics, Vol. 46, 2003.
12. Lord David, The Wealth and Poverty of Nations, W.W. Noting, New York, 1998.
13. World Development Report, World Bank, 1997.
14. World Development Lent Report, Oxford University Press, 1995.

2

Dynamics of Development Economics

"When history sleeps it sleeps in dreams
When it wakes up it appears in action".

When we look back to the dynamics of development economics, ideas surge in our mind. Past deeds induce future actions not only in thought but also in its implementation. We recollect what T.S. Eliot said, "The world turns and the time changes, but one thing remains perpetually unchanged, that is the conflict between good and evil". Tagore warns us with the words, "Oh, men, at the dawn of new age, do not waste time in vain".

When new age comes with new problems, we are forced to solve it immediately. The sense of immediacy predominates. But in an age such critical issue confronts us which makes it imperative to consider the time—past, time present and future, what things are to be done, what ways we are to traverse, all those are to be deeply pondered over in light of the present situations and its far-flung implications.

Over the ages, economic ideas and deeds based on ideas have overwhelmingly influenced life of mankind in its multiple aspects. Karl Max in his "Economic Manuscript 1855-58" in its introduction clearly states, that culture and spirituality do not depend on material base alone, they depend on social relation. That is why we observe difference in arts, and social development in different ages.

Culture, civilization and economics move hand in glove together. Culture according to Y. Cusset is a world view which saves the mankind from impending disaster. This sense of value may not be same in all its aspects; priority changes and it is the most important determinant of changes.

The world has experienced numerous changes over ages. Right from the dawn of civilization, distinct changes in social and economic relations have taken place. And nobody knows what future shape it would take. As an upshot of dialectic relations prevailing in a situation, new ideas and new actions emerge. Economic theory predicting new development appears. Over the ages, number of epoch making thought waves involving economy, society and culture have spread on the Earth.

From the nomadic state to a settled habitation, mankind has moved with the growth of population and a desire to avoid the pains of constant movement. Food gathering from forest plants being inadequate and uncertain, man started cultivating food grains. Agriculture as an art of living assumed greater significance. This continued till the end of the 17th century when industrial revolution took place. According to Alvin Toffler, "civilization based on agriculture was the first and foremost wave of culture. The next epoch making wave of culture was industrial revolution. Conflict between agriculture-based civilization and industrial civilization was inevitable. Spreads of industrialization changed the prevailing philosophy of life, sense of value in the world".

Agricultural civilization was village-based; industrial civilization is urban-based. In agricultural civilization, there was intimacy, cooperation and close link between individuals. Production was need-based. Small business and industry served the purpose of the rural people; staying in close proximity, individuals developed intimate relationships among themselves. Spread of individual culture developed alienation among individuals. Specialization in place of generalization prevented development of total personality of a man. Marx and Engels in their "Communist Manifesto" in 1848 wrote, "naked self-interest and the cruel monetary transaction constituted the relationship between man and man". Industrial civilization was based on the following principles: (i) standard of production, (ii) specialization, (iii) concentration of production, (iv) maximization of profit and (v) synchronisation of production methods and relation.

The craze for economic development and effort for its realization led to the following according to Kuznets: (i) rapid increase in production and population, (ii) rise in productivity, (iii) change in infrastructure, (iv) social change–urbanization and secularism, (v) revolution in transport, and (vi) inequality in development.

In the developed countries the changes most revealing were: (a) dynamism in management and spread of the influence of economic manager on politics and administration, (b) development of technology changing the character and size of labour, employment and change in class formation, wide circulation of information and consumption among people, and (c) increase of the powers of the organized labour.

The new labour class is involved both in conflict and co-operation with the managerial class. The power of the managerial class has gone up and that of the labour class has declined.

Trotsky in 1930 and Djilas later spoke of the tremendous power of the new managerial class. In this age technocrats had assumed supreme power. The industrial society has become stratified. On the upper layer there were high intellectuals who assume power to plan and invest, on the second layer there were middle rank intellectuals administering and monitoring the plan and at the lowest level were those who carry out the order.

As per Alvin Toffler, the second wave of civilization started losing its influence by 1955. In its place, a third wave raised its head. The character of this wave reveals the participation of labour and consumers in management of industry and business. Howard Surman observed that the developed nations would have remained at 1928-30 development level, if they were not helped by imperialism.

This was also the view of Dr. Ram Manohar Lohia who expounded the thesis that the western capitalism was fed by imperialistic exploitation. With the third world countries becoming independent, the developed nations started depending on their own resources and market. The exhaustion of non-renewable natural resources has forced to search for new sources of energy—solar and atomic. Information technology and computer and internet have helped decentralization instead of centralized production. Rise of co-operation and labour organization in US was believed to check the exploitative power of large producers.

The countervailing powers mentioned by Galbraith did produce the desired results. But shrewd manoeuvre of the MNCs has created a new wave of thought which ushered in neo-imperialism in the form of globalization. The opening up of the developing economies to the activities of the big financial and industrial powers aggravated the problems of poverty, unemployment and inequality along with ecological imbalance whose solution poses a formidable challenge.

The 1st Industrial Revolution occurred towards the end of 18th century in England. It spread to other European countries and US subsequently. Adam Smith and Karl Marx have elaborately and deeply discussed the character and implication of this Industrial Revolution. This also attracted some of the developing countries. Why not others? The answer lies in the fact that there is no flawless single unchangeable eternal path of development. The development path changes with time, country and environment. There are reasons why the earlier method of industrialization is not acceptable at present.

John Naisbiu, in his book, "Mega Trend" has concluded that there are seven waves of evolution, starting from the time human beings left the African Savannah as animal hunters until they steeped into the first virtual reality machine. This process started in 40,000 BC with the language breakthrough (40,000 BC); Wave 2 propelled the agricultural revolution (5000 BC-1500 AD); Wave 3 incubated the industrial revolution (1500-1940); Wave 4 was all about the transport and telecommunication revolution (1850-1975); Wave 5 was the computational and electro chemical revolution (1940-1975); Wave 6 set the platform for the Network Era (1975-2002). We are currently living in the Wave 7, which started in 2002, and it is all about knowledge and collaboration.

Changes in the 20th Century and Their Impact

In 20th century, three momentous events occurred—First British Imperialism and other colonialism collapsed. Second after, WW II such weapons of destructions were invented whose impact on industrialization was continuous and far-reaching. Third the poison of pollution spread fast.

The path of first Industrial Revolution was overcome by England and others by the help of their imperial and colonial connection. Food materials and capital were imported from colonies. Now it is impossible and undesirable for many countries to move on an imperial path.

The developed countries have smaller portion of world population but enjoy major portion of wealth. Hence, development path has to be different, may be equity holds the key to the future. With equity, comes democracy and self-reliance.

Even in the West, the 1st phase of Industrial Revolution was not a happy event. The path the ruling class chose was not to ameliorate the condition of the common people but to wield imperial power to acquire wealth. The struggle for power had impact on the pattern of industrialization in the entire 20th Century.

The disastrous consequence on civilization of War preparation in quest of power led to movement for peace. Power of the state and militarization were linked with industrialization. The voice raised by Kumarappa and Sumacher appears relevant. Gandhi's observation that the Earth has sufficient to meet the needs of the world population, not the greed of the mankind appeared most relevant and was recognized as the burning issue of the day. When in 1972, the Club of Rome discussed the limit to growth the pollution of the environment has reached unbearable magnitude, Mehbub Huq advised that the society should produce such goods that would be consumed by a majority of people. Each country should invent its own methods of production and pattern of development that is appropriate to its needs and resources.

Industrial civilization was running after material prosperity. Now that a limit to its expansion is realized to be fraught with danger and impossibility, a way out for sustainable development is being sought. Scientific discovery is moving slowly but steadily in that direction. Our thought process, thinking and attitude were following material goal of industrialization. Now-a-days, a change is essential. The change would emanate from strong determination and courage. We feel the essence of human philosophy of life would show the correct path and provide requisite courage—a deeper study of this philosophy reveals as Amartya Sen observed peaceful co-existence of all isms and healthy combination of social behaviour and religious ethos.

Indian philosophy has acknowledged the greatness of the creation and expansiveness of life. The thrilling poems of Tagore and Wordsworth point to the right direction of the commingling of humility and love for nature. Chandi Das's famous words, "Man is the greatest truth, there is nothing above him". Bhima Bhoi's heart moving words, "Mo Jiban Pachhe Narke Padithau Jagat Udhar Heu" (Let my life fall in hell, but the world be saved) should govern our future thinking of development. German philosopher's warning 'knowledge without compassion is like a biblical Satan to be borne in mind forever. The messages of Budha for development of individual personality are extremely relevant now. They are: (a) give each opportunity to develop his self, (b) let individual keep close link with others for removing his self centeredness, and (c) let each acquire materials and services to live like a man. For all round development of the masses, jobs and job organizations are imperative.

It appears, to avert the disasters of present day

industrialization, a new philosophy and work pattern and life style are needed. Let us decide what sort of culture and philosophy of life we should adopt and then the pattern of economic development appropriate and necessary economic thought would follow. For sustained development of society and welfare of one and all, integration of economics, culture and civilization is indispensable.

With the advent of industrial revolution control over nature was the propelling goal. Now cooperation with nature is a direct need. We are to move in quest of new technology, the quest necessarily calls for alternative to globalization. The philosophy that forces present itself for acceptance is not opposition but co-operation, not immediate gains but future sustenance, not greed but sacrifice.

We need towns and villages both residing side by side. This goal should guide us to create development of new pattern of industrialization and technology.

3

A New Look at Economic Development

Development means development of the total being of mankind. The recent crisis is a reminder of our neglect of the various aspects of human development not only of the present but also of the future generations. With change in time, society and environment undergo changes and that makes it imperative to change our views on social, political, economic and cultural aspects. Facing a challenge boldly and successfully shapes civilization. To foresee the challenges likely to come is no doubt an act of wisdom. But in a world where countries come closer and closer with passage of time, diverse interests and thinking are sure to create conflict at times. Resolution of the conflict is definitely a Herculean task. Yet, when actual crisis appears, right thinking statesmen of the world make concerted cooperative effort to reduce the impact of the crisis as quickly as possible.

The crises that have engulfed the entire world and affect different countries in different degrees comprise:

1. Impact of rapid globalization.
2. Clash of civilizations.
3. Ecological imbalance.
4. Conflict of ideologies.

The abovementioned crises are not isolated phenomenas, they are interlinked. Their refutation requires an integrated inclusive approach.

Most countries, particularly the developing ones, attribute the present malady to the speed at which globalization has spread in recent years. The driving force of globalization is surely economic in nature. Social scientists point out that globalization has moved in four phases. The first phase of globalization appeared in the 15th and 16th centuries with navigation and mercantile trade. The second phase, the most powerful phase occurred in the 18th century with Industrial Revolution. The third phase took place in 1970s with Asian countries prospering at amazing rate and increasing its trade substantially with Europe and America. The fourth phase since 1990s is associated with information technology revolution promoting convergence of cultures. The rapidity with which the final phase of globalization moves and the multifarious impacts it makes are not easily and simultaneously absorbed by all countries and all sections of people in a country. The malady is unequal distribution of its benefits, let aside the evil impact.

Since long, there continues to remain a simmering conflict between the predominantly Christian and Muslim countries. The clash is historical and religious. In recent years, the clash has been aggravated by some Christian countries attempting to grab the oil products of the Muslim world. Samuel P. Huntington in his famous book, "The Clash of Civilizations and the Remaking of World Order" has pointed out the opposition of the Muslim world to western worlds and its challenges to western dominance. The clash of civilizations in his view is the greatest threat to world peace and an international order based on peaceful coexistence of civilization is the surest safeguard against world war. Religious fundamentalism and economic deprivation are the root cause of terrorism which is now a grave concern.

Again, ecological imbalance poses a threat to the very existence of mankind on the planet. Ecological as well as social disaster can be attributed to our greed for accumulation of wealth and maximization of profit. We ignore Gandhi's warning, "The Earth has enough to feed us but not enough to meet our greed". The other day Dr. R.K. Pachauri observed that we have exceeded the capacity of Earth by 25 percent and this has been for the last two decades. According to him, by 2025, three billion people will be in water stress and thanks to the increasing global warming there will be 30 percent reduction in crop yield by 2002 in Central and South Asia and 50 percent drop in Africa. The challenge is to resolve conflicting requirements—rapid economic growth on one hand and balancing with sustainable use of natural resources, given the rising population, fragility of natural resources and low subsistence level of majority people.

With growing consciousness and thinking power of man, there has emerged conflict between ideologies, political and economic. The most disturbing conflict on political front is between dictatorship and democracy and on economic front between capitalism and socialism. The majority of people have now preferred democracy to dictatorship. Yet, sometimes some countries compelled by circumstances have embraced dictatorship. The history of conflict between capitalism and socialism is a chequered one—it is more fascinating and widely embracing.

In the early stage of Industrial Revolution and capitalist growth, the miseries of the working class invited new thinking on economic regulations. Socialism with state regulation attracted the common man.

The trend of growth of economies may be different in differ stages. It is nevertheless undeniable that capitalism and socialism with their various shades continue to stay. Capitalism has been rendered tolerable and socially acceptable with judicious regulation; socialism has allowed certain degree of capitalist production to infuse the spirit of innovation and competitiveness into body economies. Capitalism has the inner urge, to go on maximizing profit. Free economy is vulnerable to instability, inequality and unemployment. Checking the rudderless move of capitalism in the interest of the entire society is the prime moral responsibility of the state.

Occasional crisis in a free economy is a characteristic feature. The crisis occurs due to: (i) conflict between private and social interests, (ii) imbalance between financial sector and real sector, (iii) supply and demand imbalance in monetary and non-monetary sectors, and (iv) crisis of confidence amongst the economic players.

Boom and bust being linked up with the psychology of the big producers, businessmen and investors in stock market, judicious intervention of the authorities is indispensable. State with the help of the experts has to probe into the causes of the crisis and locate the forces behind it and take appropriate action to resolve the crisis.

In a democracy reconciliation of conflicting interests poses problems to the planners. Cautions and innovative approach is needed for the purpose. Amicable settlement of the issues arising at the time of development or hard steps to avert crisis necessitate proper understanding of the social and political forces and their combinations i.e. political power structure.

Twenty five years back Pranab Bardhan, identified the capitalists, the rich farmers and the bureaucracy as the three dominant classes competing and aligning with one another within a political space supervised by a relatively autonomous state. The changes introduced since 1990s transformed the framework of class dominance. There has been larger entry into the capitalist class. Partha Chatterjee divides the State population into three groups like civil society, political society and marginalized people. The civil society consists of corporate capitalists seeking maximization of profit, bureaucracy and rich farmers, political society consists of workers belonging to the vast informal sectors, street vendors etc. constituting non-corporate capitalists seeking livelihood and the marginalized sections comprising landless agricultural labours and *Adivasis*. Their interests very often clash. Hence, consensus on a developmental project needs careful and sympathetic handling.

In view of the changing situations all over the world, it may be suggested that a new look at development, based on proper insight into socio political forces operating is warranted. The 'new look' would have the following components: (i) continuous study of changing social and political forces, (ii) visualizing crisis imminent and taking preventive measures in advance, (iii) acquiring effective crisis management weapons on the basis of deep study of environmental, monetary and psychological issues, (iv) growth with a humane face, inclusive growth be stressed, and (v) checkmating consumerism and developing an attitude of peaceful and friendly living.

Above all, Kennedy's note of optimism that 'tomorrow can be better than today and that every one of us has a personal and moral responsibility to make it' should be our guiding principle.

4

Culture and Economic Development

There is a symbiotic relationship between culture and economic development. Culture of a nation influences its economic development and the latter moulds the former. Though with the passage of time the connotations of culture and economic development are undergoing changes, there are certain features which are fundamental to culture and development. The interactions between the two are slow and subtle and become perceptible after a considerable period of time. The mutual repercussions are perceived on the basis of definite concepts of culture and development.

Though it is difficult to define culture of a nation fully and correctly, yet, every citizen has a widely acceptable notion about his country's culture. Culture of a country is considered as the social and spiritual attitude based on heritage and tradition that influences conduct, behaviour and thinking of a man. Common aspirations of the people, higher values, definite aesthetic sense, a country-wide common fundamental social institutions, sweet memory of the past victory and defeat all combined constitute culture of a nation.

Art, religion, common aspiration and mass action based upon them reflect value judgements of the people and these constitute culture.

Culture is distinct from civilization. Civilization consists' of the goods that sustain life in an age. It is external to man and entails, clothing, food, transport and other materials of life. Culture on the other hand consists of the inner objects of life, spiritual, intellectual and aesthetic ideas and feelings. It is of course true that men's idea and ideology indirectly influence production and consumption of goods. A good deal of similarities between the civilizations of different countries are visible, but not so in regard to culture.

Economic development implies process of change, change in economic activities, production distribution and exchange. It covers change in: (a) factor supply, (b) supply of output and (c) structure of demand for products. "Economic development is a process whereby an economy's real national income increases over a long period of time", say Meir and Baldwin. To Schumpeter, economic development means discontinuous technological change bringing in goods, and new techniques of production and sources of new supply of raw materials and markets and forms of organizations. Economic development is a function of number of variables, social, cultural, political and financial. It is a process which is governed by existing socio-economic struggle and also influences its change.

Kaldor observes, "study of the dynamics of economic growth leads, beyond the analysis of economic factors to a study of psychological and sociological determinants of these factors. It was the emergence of the outlook typical of the capitalist entrepreneur which gave rise to modern capitalism, rather than the other way round and in countries where capitalist development lags the explanation is to be sought in the persistence of attitude incompatible with such development notably in the traditional attitude of the peasantry". The traditional attitude of the peasantry is rooted to the cultural traits handed over from generations to generations.

Social behaviour and psychological characteristics of backward nation account for the economic backwardness. The principle of 'ascription' particularism instead of achievement and universalism, attitude of self-orientation or ego centeredness, lack of objective consideration governing the economic decisions in the underdeveloped countries are not conducive to economic growth. The character and value of life springing from certain, social quality and environmental conditions get institutionalized in course of time and this leads to the evolution of a particular pattern of social relationship.

These social institutions affect the social behaviour. If the institutions become fossilized, the society becomes tradition-bound and lacks in dynamism. History gives enough evidence of social institutions influencing economic development—one way or the other. The slow growth of the economy of France as compared to the neighbouring countries is attributed to the social rigidities which hampered the flow of men and resources into productive enterprises. The school of functionalism explains social changes in terms of inter-relatedness of various processes of institutions. It assumes mutual interaction as society's basic process rather than mechanism of cause and effect.

The rigid and inflexible institutional framework—caste, class, religion, property etc. in underdeveloped countries like India, hampers economic expansion. The classical economists ignored the significance of the social institutions, but progress in growth theory is possible only if these are treated as variables.

Recent studies however have revealed that economic growth need not necessitate a universalistic protestant attitude; particularistic cultural traits of a country can be harnessed to economic progress with suitable managerial approach.

A clear perception of the goal to be pursued through planned economic development is essential. The goal, concept and measurement of economic development are undergoing changes in their importance. No more economic development is measured in terms of gross national income or per capita income. The Report of the UN Committee on Development and Planning noted, "The process of economic development is coming increasingly to be understood as process of expanding the capabilities of the people". The UNDP's Human Development Report, 1990 observed, "growth with equity is an optimal combination for generating good macro conditions needed to achieve human development". Influenced by late Mehbub Huq and Nobel Prize winner Amartya Sen's writings, economic development of the countries of the world is now measured in terms of Human Development Index constructed on the basis of expectancy of life at the time of birth, attainment of education and per capita real domestic product.

Access to health, acquisition of knowledge and entitlement to assets are being stressed as the supreme goals of development. Building up of the capability of the individual has been stressed as the main goal of development. The First Five Year Plan of India observed, "Economic planning has been viewed as an integral part of a wider process aiming not merely at the development of resources in a narrow technical sense, but the development of human faculties and the building up of an institutional framework adequate to the needs and aspiration of the people". Nehru in 1962 stressed, "Success (in planning) means raising the material, moral and spiritual level of people". When pursuit through planned development is material, moral and spiritual upliftment, the social and cultural milieu become extremely pertinent.

All development programmes aim at maximization of social welfare. Of course, conceptualization and measurement of social welfare are difficult. Yet, there has arisen consensus on certain overriding aspects of development. Fulfilment of basic human needs, equity, expansion of employment and ecological balance has been widely accepted as a prime goal of economic development. How far and in what way culture of a nation promotes or obstructs realization of the above goal is the moot question?

In spite of the spectacular growth of the world economy, the world is suffering from serious maladies of unemployment, poverty, inequality and environmental degradation. Between 1950 and 1995, world consumption expenditure has grown six times, between 1975-1995, it has grown twice yet in the present world, 1 billion people are deprived of basic consumption, 3/4th of the 4.4 billion people of the developing countries lack sanitation, 1/4th have no adequate housing, 1/5th of the children have no schooling up to 5th standard, 20 percent of the world people living in high income group account for 86 percent of the private consumption while 20 percent of the poor people account for mere 1.3 percent of the consumption.

Even in rich countries, there are 7 to 17 percent of the people who are poor. The World Development Report, 1998 revealed that people below poverty level were 11.9 percent in Thailand, 17.8 percent in Canada, 13.7 percent in US and 20 percent in UK. Unemployment in European countries and US range form 7 to 11 percent of work force. As regards environmental degradation two problems are encountered, such as: (a) pollution and waste exceeding Earth's capacity to absorb, and (b) growing deterioration of the renewable, water, soil, forest, fish and bio-diversity. Wasteful consumption of the affluent and compulsive activities of the poor are the causes of environmental degradation.

Solution of the above problems and securing healthy and decent living without endangering human existence in future warrant a new look into the pattern of economic development, mode of living and philosophy of life on a global plane. Herein comes the relevance of culture in its multifaceted colour. Rightly Gandhiji did observe, "True economics never militates against the highest ethical standard, just as all true ethics to be worth its names must at the same time be also good economics. And economics that inculcates mammon worship and enables the strong to amass wealth at the expense of the weak is a false and dismal science. It spells death". The consideration of justice has moved from utility through the availability of primary goods to the realization of basic powers—powers to fulfil one's own nutritional requirements or the necessities of clothing shelter or the ability to move about.

Indian Culture and Economic Development

If the goal is now eco-friendly growth with social justice or equity and avoidance of vulgar consumption, Indian culture is eminently compatible with such a development. It is a misconception that Indian culture is anti-materialistic and pro-ascetic. The culture of India is a judicious synthesis of the material and spiritual, the individual and social, worldly and other-worldly. Our Vedic literature, Purans and Upanisads throw enough light on the conduct of a balanced life, seeking proportionate dose of Arth, Kama, Moksh-wealth, sexual pleasure and salvation.

The four stages of life, from student's life, through the married ones to that of an ascetic, demarcates the periods of life in which different goals, learning, family nurturing, meditation and penance are to be pursued. Kautilya's Arthshastra is perhaps one of the earliest treatise on political economy, much before Adam Smith's. It does not sound exaggerated when Amartya Sen says, "There is no other literature in the world which has as much aesthetic materialistic, rationalistic writings as Sanskrit and Pali together had and have. I think that tradition of heterodoxy, of questioning is a very important part of Indian past and I think when we deny that in trying to capture India in this very limited terms of our knowledge of one part of Hindu Orthodoxy—think we make a terrible mistake".

The essence of Indian culture consists in love, sacrifice and unity—unity with nature and all human beings. Veda says:
Samano Mantra Samitis Samanam,
Samanam Mana Sahachitta mesam
Samanam Mantra gati Mantryev
Samanae ba habisha Juhomi.

You form an association—unity and love would come through. It is a way of union. Union would bring in one mind. The hearts of those committed to an ideal glow, let your mind and heart be one. Social unity of the Indians is reflected in Vedic and Buddhist literature Budha has said in Tantra Vartika "Let all the sins be on my head, and let the world be sinless".– A unique instance of love for the universe. "Tena Tyakten Bhunjiyat, Ma Gridh" says Upanisad–share the gift of the nature and do not be greedy. In the eyes of the Indians, relationship of man with nature is not of conflict but of tender love and reciprocity. Vedic prayer says, "Peace to the sky/peace to the atmosphere/peace to the Earth/peace to the water/peace to the plant/peace to the trees/peace to all beings". Atharv Veda says, "Let what I did take from thee of Earth rapidly spring and grow again, Oh, purifier, let me not pierce, through thy vitals or thy heart". Indian culture shows clear ecological orientation of evolution, an outlook extremely relevant to the present day world of ecological imbalance. Mark Arnett of Environment, Nuclear safety and Civil Protection, Brussels says, "The aim now is to match our future production and consumption patterns to what the environment can sustain in the long-run. It is but natural to think that India with its age old culture, attachment with nature should export its less consumptive happier life style".

Sukra and Kautalya emphasized agricultural development. Baudh Jatak laments the deplorable condition of the poor labourers, Panini is conscious of 'Gana', 'Puga', 'Sangh'. Kautilya speaks of state loan to established industries and monopoly of money making and licence to external trade. Thus, our culture as reflected through literature and glorious history of arts and crafts displays rational and societal approach to economic progress. It is wrong to think that Indian culture is a disincentive to economic development. Rather, it presents a balanced view to economic matter both from individual and social, short-run and long-run point of view.

The culture of Orissa too is very much pro-nature. Its culture and religion embodied in Jagannath cult synthesises, Dravidian Aryan and tribal cultural traits and ethics idealises peaceful contented life in harmony with nature and all beings around. Where else can a rustic saint sing, "let my life be in hell, let the humanity have salvation".

Tribals constitute a sizeable proportion of Orissa's population. Tribal groups are culturally very self-conscious— they are proud of their tradition. Their idea of happy and good life is based on friction-free and balanced relationship and social interaction with other members in the family and society. Over the years no doubt there has been some assimilation of tribal and non-tribal culture. But of late, awareness of the guarantee of equal rights and social status has pulled away the tribal from the process of Hinduisation towards revivalism of their own cultural systems with an orientation of modernization.

Conclusion

In light of the above discourse and the recent findings that appropriate management approach can put a political or cultural trait to economically productive use, it may be concluded that our culture does not stand on the way of economic progress, rather it indicates a proper and balanced approach to the issues of production, consumption and man's relationship with others and the grand nature. Marx in Grundrisse wrote, "while economists tend to assume that each person has his private interest in mind and nothing else, in fact, the point is rather that private interest is itself already a socially determined interest". Values and ideology determined by society are incorporated in the individual perception of interest and reflected in behaviours.

Further, when freedom is taken as main goal utility or happiness, it cannot be the criterion of progress since the two generally will not coincide. Cultural contents of life being a sensitive base of individual and social life development programmes have to pay due regard to these which constitute the sentiments of individuals. Thus, it is necessary that planners and policymakers should address the issue of interaction between culture and development. On no count external vulgar culture following globalization should be allowed to distort the native culture and sap its vital cementing force through irrational consumption. A correct effective economic perception based on totality of society, culture, social structure religious, fervour and ethnic characteristics is essential.

5

The Concept of Economic Justice

The idea of justice has broadened and entered many a field including economic field with the growth of civilization and diversity and complexity of earning a livelihood in an organized society. Etymologically, the word justice is derived from the word 'jus' which is connected with the Latin word *jungree* which means primarily joining or fitting and therefore also 'binding'. [1] It conveys the idea of valid custom to which any citizen can appeal and which is recognized and can be enforced by human authority. 'Jus' in its developed form is 'a body of binding or obliging rules which however they have been made, whether by the growth of valid custom or by legislative enactment or otherwise the courts recognize as binding and not only recognize but also enforce'. [2]

Justice no doubt encircles a set of rules or law which are statutory. But there is also a law which expresses ideal values called 'jus naturale', that is law imposed on mankind by common human nature that is by reason in response to human needs and instincts.

There may be sometimes conflict between positive law and natural law. But in most of the cases, they conform to each other. Thus, it is said that authority gives validity to law and justice gives it value. A civilized society seeking higher values must make effort to ensure justice to its citizens in all spheres. Economics being the vital aspect of human life, concept of justice and its realization have become an increasing concern of developing and developed countries.

Ramifications of the Concept
The idea of the word 'jus' or 'Justus' and 'Justitia' is the idea of joining or fitting. Primarily, the idea of joining referred

to relation between man and man, then it referred to the relation between value and value. In an organized society, different values are pursued such as values of equality, liberty, fraternity. The relationship between them is essential for an integrated whole. In the words of Aristotle, it is "what answers to the whole of goodness being the exercise of goodness as a whole towards one's neighbour". [3] The notion of justice, the idea of right and just is said to have four sources namely religion, nature, economics and ethics.

With the development of modern industry in the 19th century in Europe, economics as the origin of the idea of justice began to be advanced; first by French and German thinkers and then by Russian revolutionaries. In Marxian theory of dominance of matter, the positive law of the state at any given juncture of economic conditions is imposed on its members by the personal authority of the class which is dominant under those conditions and the impersonal source of law is similarly the inevitable imperative imposed upon that class by its own economic interest in the given conjunctural. Only in classless society when state withers away, men become accustomed to their elementary rules of social life observance without force. [4]

Proudon deduced his notion of justice not from economic fact like Marx but from economic principles, the great principle of mutuality. The French syndecalists based their theory not on warring and colliding classes but on occupational groups complementary to one another and knit together by mutual need.

Duguit based his idea of economic justice on the principle of solidarity which has two forms viz. similarity between members of the same group and difference, members of different groups cooperating for greater production. The solidarity principle of Duguit has two imperatives: (i) one do nothing contrary to the principle of solidarity, and (ii) second cooperate as far as possible in the realization of that principle.

The above western idea of the overriding power of

economics, determining or greatly influencing the emergence of the idea of justice governing the entire society has been bitterly criticized and refuted. Economics is no doubt a powerful factor developing the concept of justice, but it is not the only factor, other factors like religion, ethics and personalities too influence economic interests and all are combined for the general purpose of tidying human relations.

The western concept of economic justice may be conveniently derived from the philosophical tenet of utilitarianism which has constituent parts like (i) consequentialism which implies rightness of action judged entirely by the goodness of the consequent state of affairs, (ii) welfarism which means the goodness of states of affairs must be judged by the goodness of the set of individual utilities in the respective states of affairs, and (iii) some ranking, i.e. goodness of any set of individual utilities must be judged entirely by their sum total. John Rawls, however, upholding maxmin principle stressed that the goodness of any set of individual utilities be judged entirely by the value of its least member i.e. the utility level of the worst off individual.

In fact, Rawls explained the principle of 'maxmin' in terms of primary goods. Rawls version of kantian concept of morality was based on the conditions of the most deprived groups of person, deprivation being defined in terms of availability of primary goods, things a rational man wants. The list of primary goods includes rights, liberties, opportunities, income and wealth and the social basis of self respect. Construction of an overall index of vectors of different goods to identify the least advantaged is a daunting problem. Rawlsian difference principle justifying greater attention to a person having less primary goods than other is insensitive to special needs of disabled, old and difference in climatic condition; even sensing the difficulty of identifying the most disadvantaged group in terms of utility and availability of primary goods as well. Sen proposes such identification on the basis of realization of certain primary powers or basic abilities, power to fulfil one's nutritional requirement and ability to move about. [5]

Right from the days of Kautilya, the period of Chandragupta, 5th Century, Indian thought on economic justice has been clearly expressed with specification in relation to the manifold duties of the king, the ruler. His famous book 'Arthastrastra' is the complete work of this kind based on the methods of observation, analysis and deduction. The administration of a country according to Chanakya is based on sacred (Dharma), current law (Vyavhara), usage (Sainsthia), and reasoning (Nyay). According to Hobbs, "the king is not allowed to have his personal likes and dislikes. A king has no personal likes, it is the likes of the subjects that should be followed by him". [6]

Kautilya enjoins upon the king the supreme duty of protecting the life of the infants, the aged, the diseased and the distressed. The parental attitude of the rulers shows his sense of justice with affection. He incorporates Mahabharata's Rajadharma and Arthasastra's financial rules in the conduct of the rulers.

The first and foremost Indian thinker who seriously thought of a healthy and balanced holistic society from political, economic and spiritual angles in the modern world context was M.K. Gandhi. His political philosophy was a fusion of individualism, idealism and socialism. Upholding democracy in a broader and realistic sense, he wished the transformation of society in which self-sufficiency, non-competition, equitable distribution and decentralized production figured prominently.

To Gandhi, individualism, socialism, democracy and non-violence were interlinked. "Democratic Government was a distant dream so long as non-violence was not recognized as a living force, an inviolable creed, not a mere policy", Gandhi said. Like the guild socialists, he was against the wage system and favoured the establishment by the workers of self-government in economic and political spheres. [7]

Gandhi was a first rate egalitarian and a socialist. An ideal society cannot be formed if the gulf between the rich and the poor is not reduced, he maintained. His idea of economic equality was that everyone would have a proper house to live in, sufficient and balanced food to eat and sufficient Khadi with which to cover himself. The essence of economic justice reflected in his statement that in cultured society man and woman know that 'no one should want anything that others cannot have without equal labour'. He stressed the concept of organic unity, where all individuals have equal importance and the rise of everyone is dependent on the rise of every other.

Gandhi learned from Gita that total commitment to social action regardless of consequences to one's self is the moral law that is consistent with the principle of truth realization through love. And love is the basis of economic justice. Gandhi believed in Ruskin's view that socially meaningful action cannot be deduced from utilitarian principles and 'balances of expediency' but by 'balance of justice' meaning in the term justice to include affection—such affection as one man owes to another. [8] Thus, Gandhi's sense of justice implies right treatment to all with love and affection. Gandhian concept of justice pertaining to all has moral, spiritual and material aspects and administration of justice in a society stands for the supreme need of removing deprivation of individuals from desirable minimum of life.

Gandhi's lofty idea of building a just and equitable society based on non-violence cooperation and trusteeship was given definite shapes in the thought and action of his two noble disciples. Jayprakash Narayan (J.P.) giving practical shape to an idea in a society in a prevailing situation and help fruition of the goal contained in it is not an easy task. It requires proper understanding of the social condition and psyche of the people and dedication to a cause. J.P. and Lohia were endowed with such talent and will power. Initially attracted towards Marxism, they innovated new paths to make the Gandhian idea of justice of reality in a poor and backward country like India.

J.P.'s quest for an ideal society induced him to traverse from Marxism to total revolution through Survoday. J.P. Stood for non-violent revolution because in his view this simultaneously accomplishes the task of changing the old order and shaping of the new together. He wanted the members of the society to practice self discipline and value socialism and willingly share and cooperate, with their fellowmen. [9]

According to J.P., true socialism, the harbinger of justice will be achieved not through the increase of state power but through decentralization of economic and political power through formation of cooperatives, small industries and Panchayats for village administration. J.P. called for 'total revolution', embodying socio-economic, moral and spiritual transformation and believed in the necessity of waging permanent revolution for ensuring perpetual justice. In his view, village concepts would be potential agency of permanent revolution.

A great theoretician and practical revolutionary, Dr. Rammonohar Lohia was more sharp and pragmatic in his approach to build-up socialism on the Gandhian line which is an ideal alternative to practicing Marxism and capitalism. His theory of equi-distance from communism and capitalism, idea of *Chaukhamba* (four pillars of governance), *Saptam Kranti*, seven revolution for realizing equity and justice in material, personal, regional, global and moral sphere are innovative ideas distinct from others and most conductive to the Indian society. Lohia dealt with not only the relation of production but also with the methods of production for establishing harmony in the society. For obvious reasons, in a populous country he championed the use of intermediate technology, labour saving in character. [10]

To him, Gandhism as a weapon against exploitation, oppression and all sorts of social and economic justice is most powerful and effective one. Lohia assimilated Gandhian principle of immediacy into the triple tasks of industrialization, people's revolution and decentralization of power. "His socialism by and large was based on humanistic foundations which sacrificed the interests neither of the individual nor of the society neither of the State nor of world". [11] Rare is such a broad, long-lasting, quite practical vision of a society which would ensure and promote peace and justice of all kinds.

Following the Indian tradition of governing society on moral principles, Amartya Sen finds justice in equitable development of individual capability and fulfilment of basic needs. While recognizing the fact that moral claims to income may originate from high marginal utility of personal income, low availability of primary goods, high labour contribution, high relational obligation or event obligation, Sen seems to put great stress on building up of a society in which all individuals would have entitlement to basic needs, minimum of food, shelter, health and capability (skill and learning) to earn his livelihood. Sen argues against the consequence—insensitive ways of characterizing moral rights and entitlements and strongly pleads for the positive aspect. He says, "Concern with positive freedoms lead directly to valuing people's capabilities and instrumentally to valuing things that enhance these capabilities". [12] Thus, Sen stands for a society that would strive for upholding justice in the sense of providing opportunity to all to acquire necessary ability to live as a free man.

Summing up, it may be stated that the concept of justice has continually unfolded with the change of society and development of knowledge. The theory of justice has been woven by the threads of religion, spirituality, morality, rationality and social necessity.

With the growing complexity of economic life, struggle for eking out one's livelihood, individual conscience and State's sense of responsibility have developed. Consequently, the need for justice in economic field has acquired significance. Theory has been moulded and enriched by the imperatives of economic regulation for a stable peaceful and prospering life for the humanity.

Right from the days of Vedas where in the hymn sings "Sarve Santu sukhinah, Surve Santu Niramaya, Sarve Bhadrani Pashyantu, Maa Kaschit Dukhma Bhavet" (Let all be happy, disease-less see good of all, let not fall misery at all'), the Indian thinking has centred round the good and happiness of all in the society and the world. The concept of economics as a force reigning society led to practical programme for administration and economic management which we come across in the sophisticated theoretical form of welfare theory of the modern writers including Amratya Sen. As the early proponents of justice in economic filed pertaining to the conditions of India of different ages, the names of Kautilya, Gandhi, Jayaprakash and Lohia stand prominent. Amartya Sen amongst the leading Indians, champions the cause of justice in a way that has captured the attention of the people of the world. Difficulties encountered in giving practical shape to his idea are at present a challenge to the developing countries.

Conflicting as may be the idea of justice and the way to realize it in the society, the authority and individual would do best by listening to the voice within, not without and believe in the wisdom of Gandhi's observation. "Let us seek the kingdom of God and his righteousness and the irrevocable promise is that everything will be added on to us. These are real economics; intertwining economics and ethics into one inseparable whole reflecting vertical multi-dimensional image of man where both material and spiritual forces need to embrace each other in the human quest for unity and wholeness. [13] This is the essence of Indian approach to the idea of economic justice.

End Notes

1. A.H.J. Greendge, Historical Introduction to the Forth Edition of Postes Gaius, p. XVI.
2. Earnest Barker, Principles of Social and Political Theory, Oxford University Press, 1954, p. 94.
3. Aristotle, Ethics Book, ch. V.2.
4. Lenin, The State of Revolution, ch.V.2.

5. Amartya Sen, Resources Value and Development, Oxford University Press, 1984, pp. 277-280.
6. Aristotle, B.K., I, ch.19, p. 39.
7. R.C. Gupta, Great Political Thinkers East and West, L.N. Agrawal, Agra, 1986, p. 64.
8. Ruskin, Unto the Last, 1886, pp. 21-22.
9. J.P. Narayan, From Socialism to Sarvodaya, pp. 31-32.
10. R.M. Lohia, Problems of Asian Socialism in the Will to Power, 1956, p. 65.
11. R.C. Gupta, Political Thinkers East and West, p. 187.
12. Amartya Sen, Resource Values and Development, p. 324.
13. Ramesh Diwas and Mark Lutz, Introduction to the book, "Essays in Gandhian Economics", Gandhi Peace Foundation, 1985, pp. 12-13.

6

Structural Reforms and the Poor

The crisis in the Indian economy in 1980s appeared in the form of acute imbalance in the balance of payments, rapid increase in external debt, inflationary pressures, growing unemployment and extensive poverty.

The problems were interrelated and interacting and they are attributed to the flaws in our planning and fiscal management.

The crisis forced the Government to adopt some radical unpleasant measures by way of fiscal adjustment to set the economy on a proper track.

This chapter attempts to: (a) highlight the nature and genesis of the crisis, (b) critically examine the efficacy of the measures taken recently to ward off the crisis, and (c) assess their impact on the poorer sections of society.

The Dismal Scenario

Notwithstanding the more than 5 percent growth rate of the economy in the Seventh Plan period, the annual price rise was 9.1 percent in 1989-90, and 12 percent in 1990-91 and it was about 15 percent in the year 1991-92.

This was said to be due to: (a) sectoral supply demand imbalance, (b) additional budgetary imposts, (c) rise in import costs, and (d) persistent accumulation of excess liquidity due to fiscal imbalance (RBI, 1990:2).

The genesis of the crisis was to be located in the severe fiscal imbalances in the economy in the recent years. The revenue account of the Centre showed a surplus from 1951 till the late 1970s except for two years.

But since 1979-80, there had been a deficit. Starting from 0.61 percent of GDP in 1979-80, the deficit grew to 3 percent of GDP as of early 1990s. The Centre had to repeatedly borrow in the capital market to provide for current expenditure that yielded no returns. As a result, the fiscal deficit of the Government, consisting of official deficit financing and loans from the open market rose from 6.9 percent of GDP in 1980-81 to 8.9 percent in 1988-89.

This was due to the fact that the Government expenditure was rising faster than its income. While total Government expenditure as a ratio to GDP had increased from 27.1 percent in 1980-81 to 36 percent in 1989-90, Government's current revenue had risen from 18.11 percent to 23.2 percent during the 1980s. Gross fiscal deficit rose from ₹ 8,887 crore in 1980-81 to ₹ 43,331 crore in 1991-91 (Government of India, 1991, RBI, 1991).

Monetary resources in the economy increased at a very high rate of above 10 percent during 1970-71 and 1983-84 while gross domestic product rose at an average rate of 3.81 percent per annum. Money supply with the people (M1) increased by 15.1 percent in 1988-89 and 22.5 percent in 1989-90.

External debt in a wider sense, comprising external assistance, loans from IMF, external commercial borrowing and NRI (FCNFR) deposit liabilities, was in excess of 20 percent of GDP. Between 1980 and 1989, the debt increased from ₹ 14,520 crore to ₹ 83,835 crore (RBI, 1989a). There was persistent imbalance in our balance of payments.

This led to a dwindling of the country's foreign exchange reserves and a burgeoning of India's external debt. The current account deficit since 1990-91 stood at ₹ 10,644 crore forming just under 3 percent of our GDP.

The factors responsible for precipitating the deficit were: (i) the more liberalized import-export policy during 1985-88, (ii) levelling off of workers remittances from abroad, (iii) plateauing of indigenous oil production in the face of continually rising domestic demand for petroleum, and (iv) the possibility of a growing intensity of exports (Government of

India, 1989). An increase in the import intensity of manufactured consumer goods had contributed significantly to the balance of payment crunch.

The sharpest increase in India's import bill in 10 years had been accounted for by the item entitled "capital goods" which increased from ₹ 1,910 crore in 1980-81 to ₹ 8,831 crore in 1989-90 (Nayak, 1991:11).

A significant tapering off of remittances from abroad had taken place in the 1980s. The FCNR deposits which grew rapidly from about ₹ 955 crore in 1985 to around ₹ 17,000 crore by July 1990 started maturing and there was some reluctance in early 1990s on the part of the depositors to renew their deposits.

The adverse effects of the trade imbalances were reflected in the precipitated fall of the country's foreign exchange reserves from ₹ 7,890 crore in 1988-89 to ₹ 5,331 crore in January 1990 and to an all-time low level of ₹ 2,300 crore in June 1991.

This threatened India's credibility as a trading nation and forced the Government to devalue the rupee by nearly 20 percent in two-stages in the course of three days in July 1991.

This trend, however, was visible from several years. From 1985-86 to 1990-91, the value of the rupee in terms of the Dollar had depreciated by 6.5 percent, in terms of the Pound by 12 percent annually.

The tax to the GDP ratio has moved up in the past four decades from about 6.69 percent in 1950-51 to about 17.7 percent in 1989-90.

For a country of India's level of development, this ratio is certainly quite creditable. The problem, however, is that the share of the direct taxes virtually stagnated during the period.

It started out at 2.47 percent of GDP in 1950-55. But after touching 3.26 percent in 1963-64, it had gone down to 2.49 percent of GDP in 1988-89.

There had been a dramatic decline in the importance of personal income tax, which composed some 21 percent of all tax revenues in 1950-51, but was down to about 5 percent of the same. Indirect taxes formed nearly 85 percent of all tax revenues.

The direct tax-GDP ratio stagnated for three reasons: (a) reduction in basic rates, (b) increase in allowances and exemptions, and (c) widespread evasion (Bhattacharya, 1991:7). Thus, the poor were taxed through indirect taxes while the share of the better off had fallen.

It was reported that 240 million persons were still in abject poverty in our country, 34 million educated youth were remaining unemployed. While GDP recorded a growth rate of around 5.5 percent, the growth rate of employment rate was only 1.5 percent.

Employment in the organized sector grew at the rate of 5.08 percent per annum in the early 1960s, at around 2.4 percent per annum during the 1977 -1983 and at 1.4 percent during 1983-88.

This was almost exclusively in the public sector. In the organized private sector, employment registered a negative growth rate of -0.2 percent during the 1983-1988 period.

As for expenditure, the compound rate of growth in plan expenditure had been only 12.8 percent per annum between 1980-81 and 1990-91 while non-plan spending rose at an annual rate of 19.4 percent. The annual increase of interest payment was 23.7 percent followed by subsidies (19.6 percent) and defence (15.9 percent).

Interest payment of the Central Government increased from ₹ 2,604 crore in 1980-81 to ₹ 21,850 crore in 1990-91. Subsidies rose from ₹ 2,028 crore in 1980-81 to ₹ 12,121 crore in 1990-91.

Exports rose at an annual rate of 47.1 percent while export subsidies rose at a rate of 21 percent in the period. Fertiliser subsidy increased at a rate of 24.2 percent per annum in 1980s (Anon, 1991).

Non-developmental expenditure as a share of total expenditure increased from 56 percent in 1984-85 to 65 percent in 1990-91. This increase had been at the cost of developmental expenditure which declined by 7.3 percentage point. Besides, the beneficiaries of subsidies were mostly from the better off sections.

For example, the debt relief of ₹ 1,500 crore in the form of loan waiver benefited the richer farmers and artisans (Datta, 1990). In addition to these visible subsidies, there was a huge amount of invisible subsidies (Mundle and Rao, 1991).

Measures Taken

Thus, one can notice that the foreign debt and internal deficit crisis was caused mainly by imports to meet the needs of the elite and for subsidies to the benefit of the rural rich. Fiscal policy has to be reoriented to cure this malaise of the economy. The Long-Term Fiscal Policy Document of 1985 noted, "The alleviation of poverty is at the centre of our plans".

However, drastic changes in fiscal approach had been forced upon us not by the needs of the poor, but by the disaster of our economy in the external sector.

In response to the dictate of the IMF, it was alleged measures had been taken marking a departure from the long-trodden path. Continuous assessment of their impact was a necessity.

Policy measures which created a furore in the country were: (a) devaluation of the rupee and loans from IMF, (b) liberalization of the trade policy, (c) move towards privatization, (d) abolition/reduction of subsidies, and (e) dear money policy pruning the budget deficit and raising interest rates etc.

In July 1991, the rupee was devalued by about 20 percent and the Government set in motion the process of obtaining US$ 5 billion to US$ 7 billion under the IMF's structural adjustment facility with all the stringent conditionalities attached to it.

In the arena of foreign trade policy, the cash compensatory

support (CCS) scheme was suspended and the replenishment licensing (REP) scheme was enlarged to cover all non-essential imports. All exports were to have a uniform REP rate of 30 percent of the freight on board (FOB) value in place of the prevailing rates ranging from 5 to 20 percent of FOB value.

New Industrial Policy

The new industrial policy (NIP) is an inherent part of the series of measures being taken by the Government for the purpose, as it claims, of unshackling "the Indian industrial economy from the webs of unnecessary bureaucratic control". It emphasized market friendliness, privatization and the opening up of the economy to foreign capital and trade.

Under the new industrial policy, industrial licensing was to be abolished for all projects except those related to security and strategic concerns, social reasons, hazardous chemicals and overriding environment reasons, and items of elitist consumption. Steel was not included in the list of industries requiring licence. This implied that the country will not have any more, anything like a planned economy.

The MRTP Act, 1970 which aimed at checking concentration of industrial power was an eyesore to a big business. It was getting diluted for the last two decades and now has its chapter III laying down the threshold of investment abolished.

The idea that the monopoly houses "should be observed carefully in matters like their expansion to make sure that such expansion was necessary on socio-economic grounds and in that process no undesirable effects on the economy were created" had been removed by this (Paranjpe, 1991:2473).

All areas except eight were thrown open to the private sector. The locational policy had been given up. Foreign investment proposals involving up to 51 percent of equity were being cleared automatically.

A specially empowered Foreign Investment Promotion Board (FIPB) became operational and considered applications for foreign investment from large international firms.

Electrical, automobile, drug industries and export trade were also thrown open to foreign capital.

Within 3 months of the declaration of the policy more than 100 letters of intent with investment of more than ₹ 1,500 crore were issued. As many as 120 foreign collaboration proposals were sanctioned. Applications for 1200 industrial units which do not require any clearance had been received and taken as approved.

The Industry Minister Prof. P.J. Kurien said, "There is no going back on industrial policy liberalization. All hurdles will be removed". But people abroad were not certain that the policies would not be rolled back by the next Government.

The NIP had substantially reduced the role of the public sector in the future development of the country.

The priority areas for the future growth of public sector had been confined to: (i) essential infrastructural goods and services, (ii) exploration and exploitation of oil and mineral resources, (iii) technology development and building-up of manufacturing capabilities in crucial areas, and (iv) manufacturing of products based on strategic considerations such as defence equipment.

Consequently, only eight industries were then exclusively in the core industrial sector and the role of the public sector had been reduced to 30 percent of what was used to be. As much as three-fourth of the industrial activity was made available to the private sector (Anon 1991a:12).

Only 18 industries (infrastructural and strategic) will be subject to compulsory licensing. More than four-fifth of Indian industries were left completely free for the entry of the private sector.

The condition of the State Level Public Sector Enterprises (SLPEs) was worse. The SLPEs accounted for 35 percent of total investment in the public sector.

Of the total public sector investment of ₹ 1,30,000 crore on March 31, 1989, the SLPEs accounted for ₹ 46,000 crore. In the same year, the SLPEs numbered 1000 against Central

Public Sector Undertakings numbering 230.

The rate of return on capital invested should be 12 percent in the case of commercial undertakings and 9 percent for promotional and developmental undertakings.

In reality, their rates of return in commercial undertakings were 0.37 percent in 1982-83, 3.90 percent in 1985-86 and 2.72 percent in 1986-87.

The rates in promotional undertakings were 2.64 percent in 1982-83 and 3.13 percent in 1986-87. It was clear from the study of SLPEs that 300 of them needed some kind of restructuring (Anon, 1991b).

The new policy recognized the urgency of inviting foreign investment, with it the advantages of technology transfers. Provisions relating to royalty payments were relaxed.

In the small-scale industry (SSI) sector, participation up to 24 percent in equity investment by industrial undertakings, Indian and foreign, was allowed to promote ancillarisation and integration with the medium and large scale sector with the hope of tackling the problem of sickness.

Data showed that 2,40,573 SSI units with an outstanding bank credit of ₹ 2,141 crore were sick in 1988.

The new industrial policy along with the reform of the export-import policy, exchange rate adjustment etc. offered a total package of liberalization policies for creating a climate for rapid industrial growth.

It was feared that the release of animal instincts of the Indian entrepreneurs may result in creation of excess capacities. But it was hoped that it would provide effective protection against shortages and scarcities.

Liberalisation and Social Obligations

However, the weakest link in the policy was reconciliation of the conflicting goals of a competitive industrial structure and protection of employment.

The new policy had thrown out new leaders and laggards. The exit policy has been vaguely worded. "A social security mechanism will be created to protect the interests of workers likely to be affected by (such) rehabilitations of PSUs as per the scrutiny of the BIFR".

The Centre promised to provide ₹ 200 crore in the first year for establishment of a National Renewal Fund for retraining and redeployment of workers. But little was said about employment generation.

Some favour doing away completely with the need for MRTP clearance before venturing into new areas of production because they claim that it only allowed the political bureaucratic big business to flourish.

But by eliminating the requirement of MRTP clearance for mergers and take-overs, it virtually provided unrestrained scope for the formation of cartels and trusts.

By allowing MRTP companies to freely invest in whatever area they like except for the licensed ones, the Government ignored the problem of concentration of capital. Little thought had been given to define the areas where foreign capital participation was to be allowed.

With market saturation, more foreign investment in automobile industry will mean fragmentation of capacity that will render a large number of existing units non-viable.

The removal of Governmental restrictions on technology may lead to a virtual fleeing of Indian entrepreneurs who are negotiating from a position of weakness.

There was no exit policy to make the pain of exit more equitable. The policy may accelerate sickness by allowing corporate raiders to take over cash-rich enterprises (Raman, 1991).

Privatisation of PSEs

The NIP has put stress on the privatization of loss-making public sector enterprises (PSEs). Despite 10 percent growth in sales, net profit of 189 PSEs declined from ₹ 3,748 crore in 1989-90 to ₹ 2,730 crore in 1990-91.

As a percentage of capital employed, their net profit

declined from 4.62 percent in 1989-90 to 2.66 percent in 1990-91. The budget suggested divestment of 20 percent of equity of select PSEs, and a capital restructuring and rehabilitation scheme under the umbrella of BIFR for chronically sick PSEs.

Privatisation may take three modalities, viz. transfer of ownership, transfer of control, and management reforms.

What modality will best suit an individual enterprise would depend on its requirements in a competitive or non-competitive environment with or without any social obligations.

In the case of loss-making enterprises in the competitive sector, the alternatives of non-divestiture will need to be explored and aimed at effecting improvements.

There should be divestiture in terms of sale of assets and of ownership transfer in case of enterprises in a competitive environment with low efficiency and low social obligations (Shourie, 1991).

Privatisation in a broader sense is the Government jettisoning a large part of its role in decision-making. The Government giving up its paternalistic duties might bring some problems in its wake. But handing over public assets to a few hands appears repugnant.

Through macro-adjustment and devaluation of the rupee, the Government had abdicated its role in boosting exports and handed over to the market the function of compensating exporters.

By withdrawing subsidy to the farmers, the State is no longer willing to play the role of encouraging agricultural production. In a sense, it is no longer willing to insulate the rural sector from the excesses of the market.

In a system where the market does not function as it ought to be, it is feared that the transition from a paternalistic to a free market form of economy is going to inflict severe hardship on those who are not in a position to face such a situation (Roman, 1991).

The performance of the industrial sector during the period

April to August 1991 had been discouraging, down to minus 2.5 percent from a healthy growth of 14.2 percent in the corresponding period in the previous year. Industrial sanction was lower by 0.2 percent at ₹ 7,041 crore.

The rupee slipped consistently by 11 percent since the devaluation of July 1991. The hopes of reforms were likely to fade (Anon, 1991c). The manufacturing industry witnessed a negative growth of 2.5 percent.

The growth of exports of manufactured goods too slowed down. In dollar terms, they went up by 8.4 percent during this period against an increase of 14.6 percent witnessed in the previous year.

The import of raw materials and intermediaries fell by 13.5 percent in the first six months of 1991-92 against a growth of 18.4 percent in the same period of 1990-91. Import of capital goods fell by 6 percent against the growth of 13.2 percent in the same period of last year (Anon, 1991d).

It was doubtful whether the NIP, an extension of the liberalization policy of the Seventh Plan would produce salutary effects on the backward States.

For example, statistics show that in Orissa, a backward State, the growth of industries in the Seventh Plan was less than that in the Sixth Plan.

During the Sixth Plan, 91 large and medium scale industries were set up with a total investment of ₹ 304 crore generating employment for 15,548 people.

But during the Seventh Plan, only 83 new such industries were set up with a total investment of ₹ 432 crore having employment potential for 12,027 people. The share of the secondary sector in net SDP which was 17.5 percent in 1987-88, came down to 15.2 percent in 1989-90.

Measures announced in the direction of privatization, and macro adjustment would have little impact on common people if the area did not touch them directly.

Privatisation in the field of transport and services would be clearly meaningful to them if the quality of service was improved.

A judicious interdependence between the State and the private sectors was an imperative. The State had to play the role of a wise regulator. But the new policy did not seem to do it. The state abdicated its role completely.

Foreign Capital and External Debt

Opening the doors wide to foreign capital is supposed to promote technological capabilities and modernization. The past history of foreign companies does not justify it. Did Philip introduce transistors in India, did I.C.I. develop fertilizer industries, and did Pepsi develop agro-based industries in India?

The argument in terms of technological transfer too is weak. It is not foreign collaboration but more investment in R and D that will promote technology. Foreign collaboration in itself is the need of the elite. Some 4,000 collaborations involving ₹ 1,000 crore in 1985-89, had catered to the needs of the elite and increased heavily the import bill and were instrumental in creating the present crisis.

The best technology and management are not uniform all over the world. India needed a type of labour intensive technology and management which foreign companies can hardly develop (Paranjpe, 1991).

The NIP displayed a fetish for growth and ignored employment. The NIP was reticent about the rectification of industrial structure from chemical based and consumer durable industries where we had neither export nor employment advantage.

The DGCI and UN Trade Statistics revealed that India's share in global exports of manufactured goods remained at 0.43 percent in 1986 and at home the share of exports in the total output of manufactured goods declined from 11.72 percent in 1978-79 to 6.97 percent in 1985-86. Devaluation and indiscriminate opening up of the economy only accentuated our external debt.

The profligacy exhibited in the consumer boom of the last decade had impinged upon our savings and increased domestic debt of the central Government from 35.6 percent of GDP in 1980-81 to 54.4 percent in 1990-91. Besides, the NIP did not refer to agro-based industries. Hence, the adjustment cost of NIP will affect employment growth.

Questionable Assumptions

The crippling cost of wages and salaries is often held responsible for the trouble of industries. This is baseless. A study shows that 100 companies of the Eastern Zone experienced a 13 percent increase in their wage bill against 20 percent rise in sales leading to fall of the share of wages from 19.4 percent to 13.3 percent of sales between 1989-90 and 1990-91 (Anon, 1991).

One has to keep in mind that liberalization is not synonymous with marketisation. The premise that India can industrialise best if it moves to the free market economy is not well-founded.

Japan and China developed industrially not because of highly competitive and non-oligopolistic conditions at home rather because of high level of concentration and centralization of capital.

Japan, South Korea and Taiwan have been marked by fierce protection and numerous barriers to the entry of foreign capital and goods. The motor force of growth has been import substitution and aggressive planning to capture the world market.

For this to be achieved in India, the elitist growth model has to be abandoned and an indigenous technology has to be created for the development of the country.

The new IMF package will greatly inhibit the indigenous development of technology, instead of encouraging it (Bidwai, 1991).

Fiscal-Monetary Measures and Their Implications

To tide over the crisis, the Government of India adopted various fiscal-monetary measures like devaluation, reduction of deficit, restructuring of tariff and tax rates, and revision of interest rates.

According to the new policy, fiscal deficit was to be reduced from 8.3 percent of GDP in 1990-91 to 6.5 percent of GDP in 1991-92.

A simulation carried out on the basis of the macroeconomic model of the Indian economy developed by NCAER to examine the impact of reduction in fiscal deficit (of 1.8 percent point) revealed that on the assumption of normal monsoons, it would lead to a reduction in the rate of growth of output by 0.6 to 1 percent, of industrial output by 1 to 1.5 percent, of the rate of inflation by 2 to 3 percent and that it will have a favourable effect on the balance of payments, though not of same magnitude.

The money supply will fall by 3 to 3.5 percent and the income of the poor will fall by a large amount than in the case of other classes. Employment in the unorganized sector will be adversely affected.

The structure of capital account has undergone changes during the last decade. In 1980, nearly 90 percent of India's outstanding debt was to official creditors and 85 percent of it was concessional.

In 1989, the official loans accounted for 61 percent of total outstanding debt and proportion of concessional loans had fallen to 47 percent.

The volume of direct foreign investment in India in 1989 was US\$ 100 million (₹ 200 crore) against China's US\$ 3.4 billion. It is observed that capital intensive protection-induced capital flow may reduce income in the recipient countries.

It is a tariff jumping variety of foreign investment. Lall and Steelen have found that welfare effects of foreign investment are negatively correlated with the degree of effective protection provided to a particular industry. Thus, investment has to be positive in terms of foreign exchange and internationally competitive.

The official interest rate increased from 2.4 percent in 1980 to 5.6 percent in 1989. Interest increased at a compound rate of 21.7 percent annum in 1980 as compared to 7.8 percent growth per annum in exports (in dollars). Debt financing of large projects is not viable because of low productivity and cost escalation due to delay.

Quick-gestation export-oriented projects are to be considered for financing through external commercial loans (Japan quoted in Anon, 1991f).

The rupee has been going down since 1985. The average annual devaluation between 1985 and 1990 works out at 6.5 percent for the Dollar and 12 percent for the Pound.

Since the mid-1980s, exports boomed at a rate of 26.3 percent per annum in rupee terms and 16.9 percent in dollar terms. But the import bill swelled up resulting in trade deficits.

Devaluation to be helpful, price elasticities of export supply plus import demand must exceed one (Marshal-Lerner thesis). This is not so in India.

The strategy of devaluation requires downward movement of the share of wages in the industrial sector or in terms of trade for the agriculture (Patnaik, 1991). Hence, the strategy entails serious redistributive consequences.

The credit policy of the RBI since October 1988 has moved in the direction of replacing direct control by remote control. The policy announced in the beginning of this year has been in alignment with the liberalization process.

No doubt, in the policy framed against the backdrop of inflation the stance is one of restraint-increase in rates of interest on deposits and advances, a ceiling of 45 percent on incremental non-goods non-export credit deposit ratio and tightening of selective credit controls.

However, there is a definite pointer to the continued thrust on liberalization and deregulation like the shifting of certificate of deposits (CDs) limits from 3 percent of 5 percent of average deposits in the previous year; relaxation of conditions relating to the issuance of commercial paper, a widening of call money market and permission to banks to set up money market mutual funds (MMMF).

In October 1988, the credit authorization scheme requiring credit limit to a party beyond a specified limit authorized by RBI was abolished. But under a new credit monitoring arrangement commercial banks are required to report to RBI about the sanctioning of the limits.

Similarly, in October 1988, the ceiling of 16.5 percent on the rate of interest on working capital was abolished but a minimum lending rate of 16 percent was introduced to avoid unhealthy competition amongst banks to attract customers.

In May 1989, a ceiling on the interest rate on inter-bank call money was removed. In October 1989, a ceiling of 15 percent interest rate on term loans by banks was removed but minimum lending rate of 15 percent was introduced.

Certificates of deposits without restrant on interest rates were introduced, the duration of the CD was specified as 91 days to one year. A corporate entity is now permitted to raise funds directly from the saver without intermediaries, the minimum rate of interest on commercial papers has been laid down at 14 percent.

Selective credit controls have been in vogue right from 1956. But the amount of credit coming under selective credit control does not form more than 2.3 percent of total credit. The costs of operation make the efforts look ridiculous.

During the last 2 decades, the basic stance of credit policy has been to encourage production-oriented advances. The security nexus was almost severed and production capacity of the borrower was given weightage.

The maximum permissible bank finance is worked out on the basis of laid-down criteria and the borrower is expected to operate within the maximum permissible bank finance. Bank governed as they are by the Indian Chore Committee norm do not entertain additional financial companies.

This has led to the proliferation of non-bank finance companies and consequent cost increase. The bias towards RRBs in licensing policy resulted in a large number of sick RRBs, with the consequent burden on society.

In July 1991, the bank rate was raised by 1 percent after a long gap of 11 years. The cash reserve ratio had already reached the statutory ceiling of 15 percent.

The credit deposit ratio fell from 67.3 percent in 1981 to 59.76 percent in 1991. Bank credit to Government sector as a share of total credit increased from 44.52 percent in 1981 to 53.85 percent in 1990. To moderate dependence of some banks on the call money market, call money interest rates were freed from April 1989.

Yet, because of the resource crunch, call money borrowing occurred. RBI raised the minimum lending rate on limits of over ₹ 2 lakh from 16.1 to 17 percent with effect from April, 13, 1991, and to 18.5 percent from July 4, 1991 and squeezed the utilization limits of borrowers of ₹ 1 crore and above with effect from May 9, 1991.

Flow of funds to the banking sector over the years has been affected by the RBI's tight money policy. The flow of funds to industry was affected by: (i) the factors affecting flow of fund to the banking sector, (ii) fall in credit deposit ratio, and (iii) marginal decline in bank credits to the commercial sector. The final blow had come in the form of an exorbitant increase in lending rate. The strained flow of capital reduced the capacity utilization of industry, leading to recession.

The purpose of credit control i.e. to contain rising prices would be achieved by the credit squeeze. To come out of the crisis, monetary measures had to be supported by consistent concrete, stable and complementary fiscal and other policies (Anon, 1991g).

Conclusion

To sum up, the crisis had been the accumulated effect of inappropriate fiscal and monetary policies operating over years. Few developing countries have adequately exploited the potential of fiscal and monetary instruments for stimulating the flow of resources to high priority areas and to discourage inessential investment (Prime, 1985).

The impact on development would be accentuated by the opening up of the new economy and the new industrial policy. Private profit and social gains do not run on the same track. The multinationals, the profit maximizing predators, can hardly be expected to do good to the country.

There were strong reasons for doubting the social beneficial prospects of a policy that sought to encourage large industry with foreign collaboration and with freedom to invest where market signals of private profitability leads them (Datta, 1991).

The results of the 1966 devaluation and the policy of liberalization in the 1980s have not been encouraging. The malaise caused by our fiscal mismanagement could hardly be cured by the IMF-World Bank dispensation. The industrialized countries who dominate them wanted to restructure the international economic order to ensure economic market.

As Secretary of the South Commission, Dr. Manmohan Singh pointed out in a report that the West was trying to push certain measures which would leave the Third World impoverished and helpless. As Finance Minister, he was doing his best to whittle down every bit of resistance he had propounded.

The past experiences of India and other developing countries and the recent trends suggest that the measures adopted i.e. devaluation, deregulation, denationalization and opening up the economy to the world market are likely to dampen growth, widen inequalities, cause hardships to the poor and increase the economic stranglehold of the West.

The root causes of our malady, the deficiencies of the archaic social and economic institutions, inappropriate pattern of investment leading to "perverse growth" are not being removed. To promote long run growth subserving the interest of the vast majority of poor people and to tide over the present crisis, the following measures may be suggested:

1. The plan pattern has to be changed giving much higher priority to agricultural development, irrigation, infrastructural development, health and education that would provide the minimum quantum of social needs to all.

2. Draft on resources for elitist demands has to be curbed and essential supplies have to be augmented.

3. Necessary reforms in land and other asset distribution, workers' participation in management and decentralized planning are to be effected.

4. Blanket freedom to the industrialists at home and abroad is disastrous. Areas of free entry are to be selected judiciously.

5. Resources are to be raised by raising direct tax revenue by bringing more people under the personal income tax net.

6. Public sector activities should be concentrated in agriculture, health, education and the private sector may be allowed to enter other fields. If the public sector intends to expand its activities, it should go to the open market and raise the resources required. Management of public enterprises should be entrusted to professional experts devoid of political interference.

7. Industrial policy reforms should address to the solution of the problem of unemployment. Modernisation of agriculture and development of small and rural industries have to be given top priority. Technology has to be evolved to promote employment and efficiency. Closer links between large and small industries have to be established.

8. There is a need for judicious fiscal and monetary coordination. Bank loans to the Government have to be curbed. A limit to the growth of money supply may be laid down at 7 percent per annum and channelling of credit to the priority sector is to be effected with proper care.

9. Subsidy on fertilizers should be restricted to the small and marginal farmers and that on food to the real poor.
10. The redistribution system has to be streamlined to ensure supply of essentials to the poor at a reasonable price.

Liberalisation does not mean marketisation and the States complete abnegation of responsibility for regulation in social interest. The state has to play an alert, cautious and well-considered role in a developing economy if growth with equity has to be promoted.

7

Manifestation of Inequalities in Different Five Year Plans

In the Constituent Assembly, Dr. B.S. Ambedkar said, "for sustenance of democracy and ensuring social justice, three things are essential viz., individual liberty, equality and fraternity. Individual liberty without equality will be control of a few over many, equality without liberty will stifle initiative, liberty and equality will be unreal without fraternity".

Kuznet suggested three criteria for analyzing size distribution of income. They are, adequacy, equity and efficiency. Adequacy and equity are related. A given quantum of income more unequally distributed implies larger number of individuals who fail to get adequate income.

Concept of Inequality

Oxford Dictionary gives three definitions of equality viz.: (i) condition of having equal dignity, rank, privilege with others, (ii) condition of being equal in power, ability achievement or excellence, and (iii) fairness, impartiality or equity.

Moral philosophers emphasize the common humanity of men in discussion with the idea of equality.

Equality is the standard of justice, and it is involved in very meaning of utility. Social utility is the main arbiter when men differ in evaluation of concrete situations in terms of criterion of justice. As per Mill, justice is a natural urge of men. According to Benthanite, justice has two aspects: (a) impartiality legal, and (b) maximum utility. The negation of the above conditions of equality is inequality.

Prof. John Rawls adopting Kant's concept of morality, judged the state of affairs of individuals taking note of the conditions of the most deprived group of persons; deprivation being defined in terms of availability of primary goods or things supposed to be wanted by a rational man (primary goods include rights, liberties, opportunities, income and wealth and the social basis of self respect).

Amartya Sen focused on primary powers to measure inequality. To quote him, "It is possible to concentrate rather on utility as such nor on the availability of primary goods, but on the realization of certain primary powers (or basic abilities) the power to fulfil ones nutritional requirements or necessities of clothing or shelter or ability to move about". The deprivation of this much entitlement marks poverty and the differences mark inequality.

The concept of poverty has three faces: (i) subsistence, (ii) inequality, and (iii) externality.

Prof. Rein said, "people must not be allowed to become so poor that they offend or are hurtful to society…We have a problem of poverty to the extent that low income creates problems for those who are not poor". The measurement of poverty is done through three approaches, namely: (a) biological approach (Rowntree), (b) inequality approach (stratification by Miller and Roby), and (c) relative deprivation (Peter Town, Aksen).

Inequality is usually defined in terms of difference in income and wealth between persons. This is inter-personal inequality. Inequality may be construed as disparity between nations and regions also. Then it is termed as international or inter-regional inequality. Inequality within a nation is the most important issue.

Measurement of Inequality: Methods

Inequality within a nation among different persons is measured in terms of income, wealth, calorie availability, primary goods or primary opportunities. On the basis of availability of these goods to different decile groups, inequality index is constructed. The index is of various types, such as Gini coefficient, range, relative mean, deviation, coefficient variation, log variance etc.

Good index of inequality should satisfy two conditions:

1. Mean- Independence: The value of inequality index should remain unchanged if everyone's income is increased or decreased by the same proportion.
2. Pigou-Dalton condition or the Principle of Transfer: This requires that any transfer of income from a richer person to the poorer person should be reflected in a reduction in the value of inequality index.

According to Planning Commission, in 1993-94, the households with average per capita monthly income consumption of less than ₹ 225.91 for rural and ₹ 265.11 for urban areas constitute households below poverty line (BPL).

S.P. Gupta put people below poverty line in 1970-71 at 55.1 percent, in 1984-85 at 72.7 percent, in 1987-88 at 34.3 percent and in 1990-91 at 35.5 percent.

N.C. Saxena Committee submitting its report for the BPL census for the 11th Plan period in the August 2008 noted that the proportion of poor on the basis of calorie norm (2100/2400) stood at 75 percent in 2004-05, much above 64.8 percent in 1983 though Planning Commission said it has fallen from 56 percent to 28 percent between 1973-74 and 2004-05.

In 1973-74, for rural areas ₹ 49 per capita p.m. and for urban areas ₹ 56.6 per capita p.m. was considered to determine poverty line. Tendulkar Committee put the urban poverty line at ₹ 538.6 and the poverty percentage of 25.7 as correct, rural poverty line was estimated at ₹ 445.7 with 41.8 percent poor.

In pre-reforms period, urban economic growth helped reduce urban poverty without any benefit to rural people. In post-reforms period, there was a positive feedback effect from urban economic growth to rural poverty reduction.

Of the 1.4 billion people living below US$ 1.25 a day in 2005 (which is international poverty line), 33 percent lived in India (456 million poor). The proportion living below US$ 1.25 a day outside China had fallen from 40 percent to 29 percent. Over 1981-2005, in India, it had fallen from 60 to 42 percent (Shining for the poor too?; Dutt and Ravillion, E.P.W. February 13, 2010).

The Millennium Development Goals Report 2009, reiterated that the number of people living in extreme poverty though decreased from 1.8 billion in 1990 to 1.4 billion in 2005, is likely to have gone up by around 75 million during the subsequent years.

The International Food Policy Research Institute (IFPRI) developed the Global Hunger Index (GHI) as a measure to determine hunger and malnutrition in a country. In GHI score, India has the 66th position among 88 developing countries.

The concept and method of poverty measurement has varied with authors. The link between calorie intake and per capita expenditure has given rise to some puzzles. As pointed out by Deaton and Dreze, "calorie intake at a given level of per capita expenditure is declining over time. The drift is sufficiently pronounced to drive down average calorie consumption in rural India in spite of some increase in real per capita expenditure. The reasons for the drift are relative prices, demographic patterns, food habits and calorie requirements".

The growing economic tension and uncertainty among farmers, and use of machine taking no care to protect soil, presence of chemicals in the food, dispelling nutrition, confuse calorie relation with per capita expenditure, food security and equality.

In recent years, there have appeared various reports of poverty on national and international platforms in terms of Human Development Index (HDI) and in terms of per capita expenditure in dollars.

It is reported that between 1993-2004 calorie deficit population rose from 58 percent to about 64 percent in urban areas and from 71 percent to 80 percent in rural areas. At the all India level calorie deficient population rose from 68 percent to 76 percent. Is it not a story of abysmal failure of anti-poverty programmes to correct nutritional deprivation and inequality?

However, two World Bank researchers Datt, G. and M. Ravallion, 2009 showed with help of head-count ratio that poverty gap ratio and squared poverty index gap over 50 years in both urban and rural areas have fallen. Urban growth in post-reforms period has reduced both urban and rural poverty. (Has India's economic growth become more pro-poor in the post economic reforms?; Washington D.C., Policy Research Working Paper, 5103, October. 2009).

Not withstanding the decline in calorie intake, the expert group headed by Suresh Tendulkar revised the estimate of poverty index for 2001-05 to 37.2 percent from the earlier official estimate of 27.5 percent and for rural India to 41.8 percent from 28.3 percent. It has left urban poverty estimate at 25.7 percent. The expert body moved away from basing of poverty estimate on nutritional norms as measured by calories intake to some broader measure of consumption of goods and services.

The group moved away from calorie norms and used prices obtained from NSS consumption expenditure survey. It would have one reference poverty line and all other poverty lines should be obtained by a PPPIST of living adjustment of this line and it incorporates more items and includes education and health. The Group took 2004-05 as urban consumption reference. There should have been more discrete cut off between the poor and non-poor. A small change in cut-off level would mean great change in poverty estimation as evident from Arjun Sengupta Committee's estimate of 77 percent. Population being poor and vulnerable is defined with a minimal poverty line of ₹ 20. The expert groups revision has reduced the underestimation in poverty estimates but it has also shown that the penumbra around these figures is large (Recounting India's Poor, Editorial EPW, December, 2009).

Poverty line expenditure was defined in a particular manner directly linked to a nutrition norm, but, subsequently a different definition was used by Tendulkar. This does not allow valid comparison of poverty ratios over time. The energy intake accessible at the all India urban poverty line had fallen to 1795 in 2004-05. Proportion of rural persons below 2100 calories which was estimated at 50.5 percent in 1993-94 by Utsa Patnaik rose to 60.5 percent by 2004-05 (Trends in urban poverty under economic reforms, 1993-94 to 2004-05; EPW, January, 2010).

A paradoxical and disturbing situation has arisen all over the world. The craze for economic growth in terms of money and material possession has led to the increase in income and wealth along with the rise of discontent and decline in real well-being.

23 high-income OECD countries feel discontented. The Human Development Report states, "Although per capita income in the OECD countries now averages US$ 20,000, surveys reveal growing insecurity and considerable dissatisfaction". In Britain, New Economic Foundation's index of sustainable economic welfare revealed that during 1975-1990, the GNP rose by about 33 percent but sustainable economic welfare fell by about 50 percent. The British Social Science Research Council in a survey covering five years found that though consumption level of the people has gone up the quality of life had gone down.

Most countries have registered an increase in life expectancy but this has been accompanied by an increase in chronic problems, physical and mental. The Director General of WHO said, "Increased longevity without quality of life is an empty prize". In Britain, general household surveys after 16 years revealed 50 percent increase in long standing disease.

In Australia, 10 percent of the people commit some form of self-harm. A study by WHO, Harvard University and the World Bank noted that China also has one of the highest average suicide rates in the world—about thrice the world. In India, inflation and rising expenditure on education and health are taking away the benefits accruing from economic growth. The standards of government hospitals and schools have deteriorated. There is stress and depression due to disruption of family. Growing inequality also causes social tension.

Beijing's Youth Daily report that 560 Chinese end their life everyday. China with 21.5 percent of world population accounts for 43.6 percent of the world's suicide. About 55.8 percent of the women who commit suicide world wide are Chinese. Nicola Tyrer writes in the Daily Telegraph, "Children who have television sets and personal computers in their bedrooms may indeed fight less, but in their isolation are possibly forgoing vital lessons of tolerance and play". The Merck Family Find observed Americans' inner desire to reduce consumption. British Social Research Council in 1970s discovered congenial home life and contentment preferable to more consumer goods amongst many people. Time has come to restrain individuals from excessive consumption as well as wealth accumulation.

The concept of threshold has been used to mark poverty line. Absolute poverty uses two methods, viz. (a) direct method—identifies the deprived as those whose food consumption does not meet thes minimum calorie and nutrition needs, and (b) income-expenditure method—identifies the deprived as those who lack the ability to meet their basic needs. It uses specification of poverty line in monetary terms such that all with a money income less than this are regarded as poor.

The distribution of household consumption expenditure has to be adjusted for household size and composition. Otherwise, there will be over or under estimation of the extent of true inequality among households and persons.

Share of the poorest 20 percent of world population in global GNP came down from 2.3 percent in 1960-1970 to 1.3 percent in 1990. In trade it came down from 1.3 percent to 0.9 percent. Increasing inequality has been a historical fact. The structural adjustment program under IMF and World Bank has not made any dent on international inequality. Some say, it has aggravated inequality.

Measurement of Inequality in Indian Plans

The Planning Commission and the Government of India has been paying due attention to the reduction of inequality in our country since long. One of the most important goals of our planning is this and for that reason it has made measurement of inequality of income and wealth, both inter-person and inter-region, from time to time. The steps in this direction may be stated as follows.

On the basis of calorie requirements of 2400 calories in rural and 2100 calories in urban areas per day per person and the consumption-expenditure survey, the Planning Commission has marked the cut-off poverty line and has estimated people below poverty line since late 1960s. It has based its estimation on NSS which was quinquennial till 1981 and thereafter become annual.

NSS (32R) and NSS (1992) reveal that bottom 30 percent of rural households' share in private consumption was 15 percent in 1977-1978 and 15.6 percent in 1987-88, top 30 percent had a share of 51.9 percent in 1977-1988 and 51.1 percent in 1987-1988 and the middle 40 percent had share remaining constant at 33.1-33.3 percent.

World Bank and the Institute of Development Studies at Sussex University studied inter-country inequality and measured the degree of inequality on the basis of share of the lowest 40 percent of population. The socialist countries had the highest degree of overall equality; lowest 40 percent population accounting for 25 percent of national income.

Regional Disparity

Inequality between states in the country is depicted in terms of per capita Income. The C.S.O. collects per capita state net products at current prices and at constant prices. The time series data indicate continuance of regional inequality, though slightly reduced and ranking of states changing. But per capita income for different states are not strictly comparable as it suffers from the following weaknesses.

1. A favourable population resource relationship may give a wrong notion of developed-undeveloped.
2. Income data reveal income generated in the region and not income accruing to the region.
3. Different states possess different levels of monetization and per capita income may not be a reliable index of development.

On account of the above considerations, other indications of development are used. For example, differences in industrial growth, agricultural growth, level of literacy, workers in manufacturing industries to total workers, P.C. of urban population to total population, mortality rate etc. are used. Acceptance of an indicator depends on: (a) value judgement, and (b) availability of data.

Combined Indicators of Development

Composite indicator is arrived at by adding up the ranks assigned to different states on the basis of different indicators. The state having minimum total rank score will be the most developed state and the state having the second minimum total rank score will be next developed state. This is the simplest method adopted by V. Nath and Ashok Mitra.

New method is to assign weights to indicator before combining them. The technique that is most popular in disparity study is principal component analysis.

S.K. Rao using 6 variables, namely, output per head, male industrial workers, consumption of industrial power, industrial output, infant death rate, literacy rate and found in early 1950s that the most developed states were West Bengal, Maharashtra, and Gujarat as well as in early 1960s. Kerala, A.P., Rajasthan, Bihar, Assam, Orissa, M.P. and U.P were the least developed during 1950s. In early 1960s, Assam, Orissa, M.P., U.P., Rajasthan, Bihar and Kerala were the least developed.

B.N. Ganguly, D.B. Gupta and Hemlata Rao too studied regional disparities using combined indicators.

Second Plan stressed the need for development of less

developed areas; Third Plan suggested setting up of basic industries in the area; Fourth Plan identified industrially backward areas. N.D.C. 1968 set five criterias to identify these areas. (i) Total per capita income and total mining and industries, (ii) number of workers in factories, per lakh of population, (iii) consumption of electricity, (iv) length of surfaced road, and (v) railway mileage per population.

Pande Committee identified backward districts and on its recommendation the Fourth Plan laid town criteria to identify backward districts on the basis of: (i) per capita food grain, commercial-crop production, (ii) ratio of agricultural labour to total population, (iii) per capita industrial output, (iv) number of factory employees per lakh of population, (v) number of persons in secondary and tertiary sector per lakh of population, (vi) consumption of electricity, and (vii) surfaced road. The Planning Commission designated 246 districts as backward.

Wanchoo Committee provided some fiscal-financial incentives such as: (a) higher development rebate, (b) exemption of corporate income, (c) exemption on import duty on plant or no excise duty for 5 years and no sales tax for 5 years, and (d) transport subsidy.

Under the Sixth Plan (1984-85), National Committee for Development of Backward Areas (NCDBA) was constituted in 1986, which recommended the strategies such as: (a) sub-plan approach, (b) project funds for local planning, (c) financial discipline —not to divert funds to developed areas, and (d) incentive for staff.

The Seventh Plan (1985-90) made stray references, stressed increase in agricultural productivity of rice, oilseeds pulses, dry farming, drought prone area development and human resource development was emphasized. The Eighth Plan ignored the issue. Planning Commission sought to solve the problem in 3 ways: (i) transfer of resources from centre to states, (ii) special area development program, and (iii) measures to promote private investment in backward areas. Central plan outlay gave 46 to 51 percent to backward states in first 5 Plans and concessional finance by institutions was also given. Yet, no success. The reasons were: (a) new states did not get help, (b) poor states did not make self-effort, (c) presence of scheduled caste and scheduled tribe population, (d) location of large project did not benefit—no spread effect, and (e) total planning—not only financial aid needed.

Though poverty declined over the decades, inequality went up. In China, poverty declined from 53 percent to 8 percent by 45 percentage points, but in India it declined by only 17 percentage points. In China, share of national income of the poorest 20 percent of population was 5.9 percent compared to 8.2 percent in India. The gini co-efficient measuring inequality between 1993-94 and 2004-05 rose from 0.25 to 0.27 in urban and 0.31 to 0.35 in rural India. In China, the gini coefficient was 0.50, the highest in the world. The increase in inequality is attributed to jobless growth, reduction in public expenditure and neglect of the unorganized sector. Edward Luke of Financial Times (London) reports that Jamsedpur steel plant of Tatas employed 85,000 workers in 1991 and produced one million tones of steel in 1991. In 2005, production rose to 5 million tones while employment fell to 44,000. According to Forbes Magazine list for 2007, the number of Indian billionaires rose from 9 in 2004 to 40 in 2007 whereas Japan had 14 and China 17 billionaires (Amit Bhaduri, EPW, April 19, 2008).

8

Economic Liberalization and Regional Imbalances

Economic liberalization as a part of the structural adjustment program (S.A.P.) cannot offer full-scale solutions to the complex problems facing LDCs like India. Empirical evidence about countries that had earlier attempted such measures also does not support unqualified optimism in this regard.

While some countries had moderate to good success within a short period, a number of others had miserably failed (Chatterjee, 1993:72).

Structural adjustment programmes through trade liberalization have the dangerous potential of initiating inflationary pressure in the economy, worsening of income distribution and increasing adjustment burden on the poorer and weaker sections of the people and unless complemented by suitable policy packages to tackle the inherent structural and institutional imbalances in the economy, the economy is likely to suffer in the long-run.

It is apprehended that trade policy reforms towards greater liberalization of the country's foreign trade regime unless complemented by the alternative policy packages aimed at removal of institutional and non-economic barriers to the operation of a free competitive market mechanism, would themselves be meaningless and may even worsen social welfare.

A policy of liberalization of trade may have important effect on its industrial output and its composition and further on agricultural productivity and level of employment, which may sharpen domestic inequality in income distribution.

Lance Taylor (1988) has shown that the optimism about

trade liberalization as a panacea to the problems of export earnings and inefficient growth of domestic industries with excess capacities cannot be justified both on empirical and theoretical grounds.

The neo-Marxists think that this liberalization policy primarily aims at penetration of imperialist dominance in the peripheral nations and exploitation on a global scale.

Liberal industrial policy allowing licence to the industrialists to invest as they like and encouraging international capital flow have bearing on the development of the entire economy and its various regions as well.

The impact of the liberalization on different countries in the international field has been non-uniform because the receptivity of the countries to the ethos of unbridled competition is different.

On the same logic, the impact of the trade policy on various regions of a particular country may be uneven depending on the absorptive capacity and responsiveness of different regions.

The economic characteristics of a region consist of its resource base, quality of its population and structure of its economy. The possible and actual effects of liberalization on the above aspects constitute the total effect of the policy on the concerned economy.

It is, therefore, pertinent to assess the impact of liberalization on the regions in terms of its impact on its various occupations and various sections of the people in the region.

In other words, we may analyze the effect of liberalization on regional imbalance in terms of its response and reaction of the relevant economic variables to the liberal policy.

Liberalisation policy affects the pace and nature of industrialization of a region depending on how it reacts to the policy. Liberalization promotes competition, which is expected to raise factor productivity, technology and management, which are the instruments of growing competitiveness.

It is a fact that the liberal policy does not make an attempt to remove the innumerable hurdles faced by small industries, small entrepreneurs, and small farmers comprising the bulk of the population. The liberalization process has neglected the interest of the small producers.

The financial sector reforms have reduced priority sector loans and their economic interests and have encouraged economic concentration.

Arun Ghosh (1995) has emphasized that the real problem of the present policy is the total neglect of the bulk of Indian producers and consumers.

Before the average Indian has acquired proper education and skill, he is forced to face unfettered competition from stronger competitors in the rush of private rent-seeking producers from outside which destroy the viability of Indian producers.

In the guise of seeking the latest technology, India is destroying indigenous research and development capability. As per the World Labour Report, 10 to 25 percent of labour in industrialized market and 25 to 50 percent in developing economies are self-employed (ILO, 1987).

The self-employed are obviously in the household industries and small farmers.

The optimism of competitiveness of the large industries to face world competition and thereby contribute much to the overall growth of the economy with distributional aspect is farfetched. .

The share of the industrial sector in India's GDP has grown from 22 to 29 percent during the last 25 years (1965-90), but the competitive ability of the industrial sector measured against other nations has remained poor.

Labour productivity in terms of value added in manufacturing in India was 617 against Brazil's 7,724, Thailand's 9,336, South Korea's 4,667, Germany's 3,820, France's 35,287 and Netherlands's 36,173 in 1986 (The World Competitiveness Report, 1990; IMD and World Economic

Forum, Switzerland).

The present level of competence of the Indian firms is a historical product of the past economic policies to serve protected domestic market.

"Unless a world class manufacturing excellence is developed by the Indian industries, it will be difficult even to survive or to meet the requirements of the domestic market" (Chandra and Shukla, 1994).

The leap frog development with technological innovation and infrastructural strength is likely to occur in richer states. This is likely to widen the gap.

Liberalization Policy and Employment

Liberalization policy may influence regional imbalance through its impact on employment generation. The occupational structure of the Indian working population is characterized by predominance of employment in primary sector.

As per 1991 census, of the total main workers, 67.53 percent were engaged in primary sector, 11.97 percent in the secondary sector and 20.50 percent in the tertiary sector.

An analysis of the percentage of main workers in different sectors state-wise roughly indicates that the poorer the state, the higher is the percentage of workers in the primary sector.

The NSS report says that organized sector employment rose by 50 percent while employment in unorganized sector nearly doubled between 1972 and 1987-88 (Vaidyanathan, 1994).

Almost 70 percent of additional non-agricultural wage employment during the period was accounted for by the unorganized sector.

The share of informal sector in total non-agricultural wage-employment rose from around 53 percent in 1972-73 to 62 percent in 1987-88.

In the initial period of structural adjustment programme, employment in formal sector is likely to fall and this leads to a rise in informal sector employment in the informal sector, characterized by poor conditions of work, low earnings and lack of social security.

So it would be an important concern of the government to see how the quality of employment can be improved (Mitra, 1994).

Increase in investment following liberal policy may result in additional employment. But there is no reason to believe that the most modern technologies with foreign capital tend to imply necessarily lower capital to labour and lower capital to output ratios.

On the other hand, the imported technology is likely to be more capital intensive leading to replacement of labour (Bramhananda, 1994).

To the extent this happens in a region, employment situation will worsen thereby causing deterioration in the economic condition of the common man.

Poverty, Inequality, and Liberalization

The liberal policy assumes: (i) that economic growth automatically results in reduction of poverty, through trickle-down effect, and (ii) that growth will be slower if redistribute measures are pursued.

The export orientation of the policy means that the gap between tradable and non-tradable goods in the agricultural sector will increase and the growth in the manufacturing sector will increase demand for workers with basic literacy and skill and the gap between skilled and unskilled workers would increase.

The additional income generated from growth accrues to those who own assets whether physical or human. Considering the fact that there are great variations of poverty levels and literacy and skill levels of people between different states, the benefit accruing to the states from the new policy would widely vary and this variation will widen the regional disparity.

Rightly, C.H. Hanumantha Rao (1995) has stressed that, "unless the task of poverty alleviation and social objectives are placed high on the national agenda, it would be difficult to prevent the market forces unleashed under the existing package of economic reforms from further marginalizing the weaker section".

States like Orissa having larger share of weaker sections (SCs, STs and OBCs) are sure to lag far behind the richer ones.

Liberalization and Economic Disparities

With stress on economic liberalization, reduction of subsidies on fertilizer has taken place and this has affected production and absorption of labour in agriculture.

Elimination of priority sector concessional bank finance will adversely affect investment in agricultural production.

The new policy seeks to cut the productivity umbrella while spearheading the market machinery. The new policy does not touch the problems of land reforms and distribution of lands above the ceiling.

Mechanized farming is now showing slow absorption of labour in the green revolution belt, whereas structural and tenancy reform is yielding higher rate of growth of output and employment in West Bengal.

The new farm policy is not properly formulated encompassing land reforms, environment protection and increased investment. The market friendly policy may raise the price of the product and reduce the real wage of agricultural labourers.

The states with large number of marginal farmers and agricultural labourers are bound to suffer due to the liberalization policy. The C.S.O. estimates that investment in agriculture was ₹ 4,636 crore in 1980-91 and ₹ 46,171 crore in 1992-93 at 1980-81 prices (Economic Times, 6th November, 1995).

J.G. Williamson (1965) observed, 'the poor countries are characterized by large and growing regional disparities and the rich countries are characterized by small and diminishing gaps".

India is a poor country displaying high and increasing degree of regional disparity. Interestingly, Punjab and Haryana, the two 'Agriculture-SSI' based states are on the top, constituting the richest states whereas Gujarat, Karnataka, Tamil Nadu and Maharashtra form the middle category states based on 'Urban-Industry', the rest form the low income states. The rate of growth since 1991 is rising but the sign of diminishing disparities is not there.

There are three groups of factors determining social development—demographic factors (birth and death rate, child and maternal mortality rate), literacy and educational attainment and income and other indicators.

Six major underdeveloped states, Bihar, Uttar Pradesh, Madhya Pradesh, Rajasthan, Orissa and Assam are poor in demographic terms.

There has been a disturbing feature of distinct decline in per capita expenditure across the states on education and medical and public health since the second half of the 1980s (EPW, 1994:1300).

The new economic policy of liberalization has slackened state's role in the field of education and health. This is sure to aggravate the socio-economic conditions of the poor states.

Studies show that the inter-state variation in trend growth has been considerably reduced since 1981-82 till 1989-90 (Dholakia, 1994). But eight states, viz., Andhra Pradesh, Jammu and Kashmir, Kerala, Manipur, Orissa, Rajasthan and Tamil Nadu have seriously lagged behind the rest.

The problems of development strategy in Bihar and Rajasthan, fluctuating agriculture in Tamil Nadu, deceleration in secondary and tertiary sectors in Kerala and decline in primary sector growth in Manipur, Jammu and Kashmir and Orissa account for the low overall growth in these states. These problems are not addressed by the liberalization policy.

Hence, it is apprehended that these states may continue to

lag behind the rest in terms of trend growth rate of GDP in future. If this happens, the regional disparity between Indian states may not be reduced.

Economic efficiency needs excellence in both hard as well as soft technology. The soft technology of management, project planning and execution, organization, marketing negotiation etc. are often the main advantages of liberalization policy. These cannot be withheld from the Indians.

The infusion of new technology even if not shared with the Indians will at least provide better products and give incentives to the Indian manufacturers.

The MNCs are expected to bring at least technology better than the existing technology (Parikh, 1996). To that extent, quality improves and costs are reduced and consumers benefit. The states will benefit accordingly as they accommodate to the foreign direct investment (FDI).

There is increasing globalization. The world trade of goods and services, which formed 25 percent of World GDP in 1970 went up to 45 percent in 1990. Capital flows accounting for 10 percent of global GDP and about 11 percent of capital formation in developing countries over 1970-1990 could be attributed to cumulative effect of capital mobility. This process cannot be stopped.

Taking advantages of the capital, flow depends on the states' effort and complementary facilities. In a federal set up where states' abilities vary, absorption of FDI is bound to vary and to that extent it would contribute to the variation in industrial and economic growth.

The real flow of foreign capital reveals that the major portion of it goes to the advanced states like Gujarat, Maharashtra, Karnataka, Tamil Nadu, Punjab and West Bengal. Other states get very negligible percentage of the total flow.

A study by IMF says that about 1.5 percent of the gap between real per capita incomes in rich and poor states was closed each year during 1961-1991. It would take about 45 years to close half the gap between the rich and the poor states.

The Report says that among the six initially poor states in 1961 (Manipur, Bihar, Orissa, Tripura, Uttar Pradesh and Madhya Pradesh), five (Manipur, Bihar, Orissa, Tripura and Uttar Pradesh) remained among the six poorest in 1991. This being the situation in the comprehensive planning period, it is doubtful how the gap will be reduced in the period of liberalization.

Conclusion

To conclude, it may be argued that regional disparity in a sense is a reflection of inter-personal disparity. The states composed of poor people are poor.

Policy of economic liberalization on the international plane has revealed disparate results, most dismal effect is on countries of Africa, sub-Sahara.

Similarly, its immediate and medium term effects are likely to be adverse on the poor states in India on following grounds.

1. Foreign capital flows more to the richer than poorer states.
2. Liberalisation neglects agricultural development by withdrawing or reducing subsidy.
3. It adversely affects small and household industries and encourages big and organized sector to compete away the small-unorganized informal sector.
4. It discourages specified direct poverty eradication programmes and thereby checks the rate of eradication of number of poor persons.
5. Its emphasis on capital intensity and modern technology discourages labour intensive method and small production units and thereby promotes unemployment.
6. Relative neglect of health, education and social service weakens the competitive strength of the states which are backward in these respects.

Hence, well considered specified measures are to be taken to checkmate the evil effects of liberalization and thereby smoothen the process of regional balances.

9

Disparities: How Much Inevitable and Desirable?

The recent growth process based on globalization is bitterly criticized for accelerating inter-regional and inter-personal disparity without perceptibly mitigating poverty. This evil impact of globalization is more pronounced in developing economies of Asia, Africa and Latin America than in the developed ones. Structural adjustment has its merits and demerits as well. Developing countries like India are devising ways of availing the merits and reducing or averting demerits. Success in this field may not be encouraging, yet, efforts are on.

Since perpetuation of poverty and widening disparity are both morally and socially undesirable and economically of doubtful merit, social scientists are engrossed in finding the relationship between the two and checkmating the contradictory trends of the growth process. With that end in view an attempt is made to highlight: (i) to what extent the present process of growth is accelerating disparity, (ii) to focus on the relationship between unequal growth and poverty accentuation, and (iii) to suggest measures necessary to prevent adverse effect on poverty-eradication and equality of the growth process.

Structural adjustment has three distinct aspects, namely globalization, liberalization and privatization. Injudicious state regulation of the economies adversely affects the competitiveness and efficiency, slows down the rate of growth, openness of the economy which has national and international implications, and unfettered privatization may loosen the states hold on the entire economy and society and may generate a sense of irresponsibility of the administrative and political machinery. Structural adjustment done in some Asian, African and Latin American countries since early 1980s had mixed impact on concerned economies. India compelled by worsening foreign exchange reserve condition and debt problem adopted a structural adjustment process from 1991. The experience in early years was most disappointing. Later on, the UNDP Report stressed on reforms with a human face and warned the governments against indifference and advised them to act as facilitator of private activities in a positive sense. Realization of the need for the continuing concern of the government for the poor and marginalized sections of the society has resulted in reconciliation of higher rate of growth with some degree of improvement in the conditions of the poor since late 1990s.

To keep the interest of the majority of the people, the common mass uppermost in mind, the noble minded economists and social scientists, go on harping on the need for inclusive growth which inter alia aims at providing more employment thereby reducing poverty and disparity.

The Nobel Laureate economist Joseph E. Stiglitz observes, "Growth must be inclusive, at least a majority of citizens must benefit. Trickle down economics does not work…an increase in GDP can actually leave most citizens worse off". [1] If most citizens are worse off, inequality must increase. In Stiglitz's view, there need not be trade off between inequality and growth.

Loosening of state control and increasing role of market forces may unfold talent and capability of some energetic and foresighted people, but it may stifle the activities of many and eliminate the weak and lead to the survival of the fittest. That is why Amartya Sen observed, "Market exchange is an essential element of man's relation. Unreasonable restriction distorts relations. But state has to pay attention to the individuals' and organizations' capacity in market exchange". [2] Speaking of globalization he added, what one does rationally, intelligently and humanely will decide its results.

The statement implies that whatever may be growth process, if carefully applied, it will leave majority unhurt while benefiting the entire economy. Maximizing welfare being the supreme goal in a democracy attempts to enrope more and more people in the development planning is definitely a task worth pursuing. Since nature has endowed different regions with different potential resources and different individuals with varying talent and capacity, development of all regions and all persons equally is impossible. It is also not desirable. Disparity in a tolerable harmless degree need not cause worries.

Equality is a protean notion. It changes its shape and assumes new forms with a ready facility. Equality in a sense is the beginning, not the end, the end depends on ourselves and on the use we make of equal conditions governed by the state. Equality is a derivative value. It is derived from the supreme value of development of personality in each alike and equal but in each along its own different like and of its separate notion. What is true of person is true of a region. It is not uniformity of development but equal opportunity for development that is aimed at.

Equality is sought on the grounds of difference of utility, derived from different level of incomes, availability of primary goods in different measures to different income earners (Rawls), or difference of primary powers i.e. basic abilities to fulfil ones urgent needs (nutrition, moving about etc.) as Sen advocated. [3] Greater entitlement of a person or a region may appear just and desirable when we rationally consider the pressing needs from as wide an angle as possible.

Claims to greater income than now available may also be based on violation of personal liberty consequent on denial of income to a person; higher labour contribution to production high relational obligation or event obligation to others. When more than one moral claims are accepted for equality, there are several non-compulsive principles competing for attention.

The question of inequality between nations is sometimes

studied treating two nations as two persons. This is not very relevant. It has to be considered from the possible policy angle. At least countries existing status-quo should not be disturbed, for worse, change has to be effected to improve the primary powers, nutrition, clothing, shelter etc. of poor disadvantaged nations. Steps should be taken keeping in view the social welfare separately for each country in nationalist terms.

Political philosophers have placed equality at a much higher platform. To Dr. Ram Manohar Lohia, equality is perhaps as high an aim of life as truth or beauty. Man has been tempted to work hard for greater fear. But direct and intuitive feeling of unity and equality gives supreme incentive and pleasure to work. Equality in its broader sense is found to be inward and outward as well as spiritual and material. Equality must therefore be grasped in all its four meanings. Material equality must mean the outward approximation among nations as well as the inward approximation within the nation. Spiritual equality must mean outward kinship as much as it means inward equanimity. [4]

Understood in this sense, it strives for greater equality and reduction of disparity—regional and personal and will contribute a lot to individual, social, national and international peace. In similar vein, Jay Prakash Narayan wrote in 1936, "If the ultimate objective is to make the masses politically and economically free to make them prosperous and happy, to free them from all manner of exploitation, to give them unfettered opportunity for development, then socialization becomes a goal to which one must irresistibly be drawn" (SWJNP18). Socialism stands for liberty and equality. Simultaneous pursuit of the two goals is the aim of an ideal state. Thus, the need for reduction in disparities.

Inequality is a neglected dimension of the neo-liberalization reform programme. But according to Birdsoll, [5] it determines the long-term sustainability of reforms programmes because: (i) inequality not only inhibits growth in countries with weak markets and governments but could even contribute towards making both weak; (ii) it undermines good public policy by undermining good collective decision-making and social institutions critical to healthy societies; (iii) across country correlation analysis report in Birdsalt (2005) indicates a low but positive correlation between inequality and the poverty head relation; (iv) inequality between regions in a federal state like India aggravates conflict between states; and (v) regional political parties forming coalition government face formidable difficulty in governance.

Disparity across the nations has been accentuated in recent years thanks to the leading roles of the MNCs backed by globalization. It is often argued that free market would optimize resource use and thereby raise the rate of growth. In fact, relationship between free markets and economic development is far more complicated and the benevolence or otherwise is critically conditioned by historical circumstances and institutions of individual country.

In Asian region, in the past three decades, nations with market-friendly policies have fared much better than nations with socialistic orientation on growth rates. In the African continent, by contrast, reforms have hardly achieved much excepting South Africa. Ideally, each country should work out its own road map using its own available expertise. Instead, there is a uniform reforms blueprint prepared under the aegis of multilateral institutions based on the so called 'Washington Consensus'.

The growth in the post-reforms period appears high from Indian standard, yet McKinsey report says the growth would have been higher if reforms would have gone far ahead. Balkrishna considers the growth as lustreless because of decline in budgetary support to capital formation in agriculture. Amartya Sen (2007) attributed the higher trajectory growth in 1970s to the impetus of increasing private investment finance, deepening public investment and declining relative price mechanism. [6]

With increasing savings, investment rates, and external

trade, India's economic growth has become quite appreciable amongst the Asian nations. The GDP growth rate in India during 2000-2004 stood at 6.9 percent compared to the world's 4.1, Bangladesh's 6.3, Pakistan's 6.4, Sri Lanka's 5.4, Indonesia's 5.1, Singapore's 8 percent, Thailand's 6.2, China's 10.1, Japan's 2.5 and Korea's 4.7 percent. The Economic Intelligence Unit (2006) projected that India will grow at the rate of 4.6 percent as against the world's 2.5 percent, China's 5.6 percent and much above other Asian nations. [7]

Growth in India and in other countries have been attributed to financial liberalization, inflow of foreign capital due to openness of the economy and due to consumption boom of some sections of the population of some countries. But it has been more and more realized in recent years that if growth is not broad-based, if it has little impact on poverty, if it pays insufficient attentions to the long term uses such as environment and national resource limitation and if the benefits of growth are increasingly cornered by a minuscule section of the population, the consequent social tensions and political instability will inevitably frustrate the growth process. [8]

The ultimate touchstone of reforms is the success it has in making a dent on the deeply entrenched poverty in India, while there is evidence to suggest that growth is a necessary condition, it is unlikely to be a sufficient condition to achieve poverty reduction. Frankel and Romer (1999) have demonstrated that in general, trade openness does have a statistically and economically significant effect on growth, suggesting that such growth has positive impact on poverty reduction. However, policy measures are needed to ensure that such an impact on growth is not accompanied by markedly increasing income inequality.

India accounted for 2.6 percent of world's commercial service trade while China accounted for 4 percent India's merchandise export valued at US$ 76.6 billion against China's US$ 593.3 billion in 2004 when world export was valued at

US$ 9,163 billion. India has to go a long way to spread its trade for deriving growth benefit. But in this effort it should not lose sight of social implications.

Poverty, unemployment and inequality being intimately connected with one another and having profound impact on individual and social life, it is pertinent to throw light on these.

The poverty ratio increase between 1999-2000 and 2004-05 is a reflection of the fact that the results of the 55th NSS Round are not comparable to that of the 50th. Over the 11 years span, the decline in poverty was only 8 percent. Average annual decline was 0.7 percent. Chen and Ravellion (2004), using poverty line definition (US$ 1.08 a day per person at 1993 PPP) obtained 34.7 percent HCR of poverty in India. Poverty in India has been consistently higher than that in South Asia generally.

Juxtaposed with the issue of poverty is that of unemployment which is likely to prove the achilles heel of the reforms process.

Increase in unemployment in LDC may occur due to the following reasons. (a) A decline in terms of trade owing to low level of demand for LDC exports in advanced countries. (b) Corporate restructuring and acquisition. (c) Rapid growth of labour saving technology of the multinationals. (d) Global spread of new technologies makes the least educated people unemployable. (e) Structural adjustment programme aiming at fiscal consolidation encourages cuts in social spending. Unemployment is on increase all over the world because of capital intensity of new technology. Different rates of population growth and ups and downs in economies because of varying degrees of response to the challenges of global competition may cause growth of unemployment at varying rates.

While poverty and unemployment directly hurt the body and mind of the deprived, inequality, regional or personal wounds the feeling and distorts thinking of the people who are socially conscious and mentally alert. The most perplexing phenomenon is that a notion is formed that the process of development which widens disparity also aggravates poverty and unemployment. No doubt, it is statistically unconvincing to prove the nexus between poverty unemployment and inequality.

The study by Ahluwalia (2002) covering 14 major states showed a sharp rise in gini coefficient from 0.175 (1991-92) to 0.233 (1998-99) based on the state domestic product per capita. Deaton and Dreze (2002) reiterate similar conclusions but were based on per capita consumption across states. [9]

Studies of Mundle and Tulsidhar (1998), Ravellion and Dutt (1999) and Jha (2000) reveal that in 1990s, both rural and urban inequality has moderately risen, compared to the previous two decades. The widening of the rural-urban income gap has implied significant increase in overall inequality. [10]

Countries embarking on neo-liberalization programmes experience increase in inequality due to the following reasons:

1. The policy has reinforced the existing land concentration and promotes unequal access to education and health. Stress on privatization leads to opening up of private educational institutions and health centres which is benefiting the better off and reducing such service to the poor by the state.
2. Emphasis on new technology contributes to the demand for skilled workers and neglect of unskilled labour which widens wage differentials.
3. Often inappropriate choice of technology leads to scarcity rent for skilled workers. Mobility of capital and labour favours the growth of an economy having congenial atmosphere, political-social, disfavouring hostile countries.
4. Labour market reforms like relaxation of safety norms, reducing job security and weakening collective bargaining to attract foreign investment have worsened the condition of the common workers in general. Tax reduction on income and property and the consequent rise in indirect tax has helped the rich and hurt the poor.

Deregulation of the economy has led to investment in real estates and other fields where accrual of income is very high. Financial reforms raising salaries of bank and insurance services compared to other pay scales has also accounted for income inequality.

Capital flows are likely to lead to real exchange rate appreciation, which shifts resources to non-tradable sector and encourages, sub-contracting and wage cuts in tradable sectors to preserve profit margins. Increasing openness of the capital account increases the vulnerability of the domestic economy to financial crisis. These crises have pronounced disequalising effects in countries with weak institutions and social safety mechanisms.

Galbraith and Lu document that in Latin America, financial crisis raised inequality by 73 percent and in the Asian crisis inequality rose by 62 percent. [11]

Evidence of changing inequality in India is scanty. Radhakrishna and Panda's study shows an increasing Gini Coefficient in urban sector of 2 states and decline in rural sector of four states.

That 47.0 percent children in the age group 1-3 years were found to be under-nourished, about two fifth of the adult population were found to be suffering from chronic energy deficiency (CED), speaks of poverty and inequality in our country. Our Human Development Index (HDI) though has risen from 0.438 in 1980 to 0.513 in 1990 and to 0.602 in 2003, yet India ranks 127 compared to China's rank of 85 (HDI 0.755) and Mexico's 53 (HDI 0.814).

Poverty ratio (HCR) declined in India from 35.97 percent in 1993-94 to 27.5 percent in 2004-05, the average decline in the incidence of poverty being 0.77 percent per annum. But difference in regional poverty ratios continues to worry. The decline rate varies from 0.20 percent to 1.92 percent. Six states viz. Bihar, M.P., Maharastra, Orissa, Rajasthan, and U.P. where the share of poor was 62 percent in 1993-94 rose to 69.02 percent in 2004-05 whereas population share remained constant at 54 percent. Extreme poor whose per capita consumption was less than 75 percent of state specific poverty line, declined from 15.54 percent to 10.32 percent between 1993-94 and 2004-05.

There has been a decline in extremely poor from 31 to 22 percent within 10 years from 1993 to 2004. Yet, about 41 percent of people survived on an average expenditure of less than of ₹ 15 per day in 2004-05 despite higher growth rate. Obviously, the growth process has not been much inclusive. Unless and until the growth is inclusive, the disparity between persons and regions will continue to widen. Decline in poverty ratio per annum has been different in different states. Rich states like Gujarat, Maharashtra and Karnataka have experienced average decline in poverty ratio less than the Indian average.

Pro-poor growth strategy is needed to generate income for the poor. For this, stress has to be given on production of basic goods. The role of civil society organization and Panchayat Raj Institutions (PRIs) in alleviating poverty in Andhra Pradesh has been exemplary. The expanding role of civil society groups should not provide an escape route to the government.

Study made by Arvind Virmani (EPW, 2008) shows that IPC increase in the per capita GDP results in 1 percent reduction in poverty rate. It is also found that 1 percent growth in agricultural product reduces poverty by 0.45 percent. The share of the bottom 40 percent of population in consumption also explains poverty differences. [12] Hence, development efforts need be directed towards increase in GDP through improvement of agriculture and inclusion of bottom 40 percent people in development process through appropriate education.

Private sector is now playing a greater role in the growth process. The share of corporate sector in GDP has risen from 5.5 percent in 2001-02 to 12.4 percent in 2006-07. The NSS Report of the National Commission for Enterprises in the Unorganized Sector (2001-2007) shows that 77 percent of the population consume less than ₹ 20 per person per day. There is rising disparity in China, Russia and the US. The rising disparity causes a tendency for under-consumption to aggravate.

Public sector investment is essential in sectors producing public services. Government's tariff and tax policy should be directed towards enhancement of public investment in sectors like health education and other infrastructure like roads, transport and electricity.

Services sector share in domestic product has gone up from 42 percent in 1991-92 to 54.7 percent in 2006-07. Inclusion of more and more people in this sector will go a long way to reduce disparity.

End Notes

1. Joseph E. Stiglitz, Turn Left for Sustainable Growth, The Economic Times, 18.8.08.
2. A. Sen, Development as Freedom, 2000.
3. A. Sen, Resources, Values and Development, Oxford University Press, 1984, p. 281.
4. Ram Manohar Lohia, The Meaning of Equality-Marx, Gandhi and Socialism, 1978, p. 241.
5. Birdball, N. (2005), Why Inequality Matters in a Globalizing World, Wider Annual Lecture.
6. McKinsey, Global Institute (2001), India-The Growth Imperative; Balkrishna P. (2005), Macro-economic Policy and Economic Growth in the 1990s, EPW, September, pp. 3969-3970; Sen, A. Sen and Himanshu (2004), Poverty Inequality in India, EPW, 18th September, 2007.
7. Mukul G. Asher, India's Rising Role in Asia, I.E.J., April-June 2007, pp. 21-24.
8. Dilip M. Nanchane, The Decades of Structural Reforms in India-A Balance Sheet, *Arth Vijnana*, September-December 2007, p. 182.
9. Ahhawalia, M.S. (2002), State-level Performance under Economics Reforms in India; Economic Policy Reforms and Indian Economy, Anne Crueger, Chicago University, Deaton, A.P.J. Dreje (2002), Poverty and Inequality in India-A Re-examination, EPW, 7th September, pp. 3729-3748.

10. Mundle and V. Tulsidhar (1998), Adjustment and Distribution-The Indian Experience, Paper No.17, Asian Development Bank.
11. Dilip M. Nanchane, op cit., p.190.
12. Arvind Virmani, Growth and Poverty-Policy Implications for Lagging States, EPW, January 12, 2008.

10

Changing International Scenario and the Poor in India

The international scenario has undergone perceptible change since the collapse of the Soviet Union in 1989. In a unipolar world, IMF, World Bank and WTO at the instance of USA and some developed countries are influencing the economic policies and conditions of the developing countries. The policy of globalization, liberalization and privatization imposed on the member countries by the international organizations has affected adversely the economic conditions of the poor, the small marginal farmers and unorganized labour by undermining the protective and ameliorative role of the state.

Here, it is analysed, how the rate of decline of poverty has come down in India in 1990s due to the new economic policy and openness of the Indian economy. It pleads that unless the developing countries are alert about the menace of unchecked capitalism and take appropriate steps to strengthen the bases of their domestic economies and streamline their administration and reform social organizations and build up right type of motivations of the common people, more openness and liberalizations of the economy will not bring in the desirable prosperity to alleviate poverty.

In the period when globalization and liberalization reign supreme in the international field, three international institutions namely, IMF, IBRD and WTO wield tremendous influence on the economies of the countries of the world. These three institutions constitute the 'trinity' of which WTO is the latest incarnation of GATT, which is assigned a vital role in the international world.

Revolution in information technology (IT) and

communication has accelerated openness to trade and investment. Openness affects productivity and efficiency by making available new and cheaper capital goods bringing in new ideas and imposing market discipline.

Openness to trade affects income distribution by increasing the export of the internationally low skill-product from the developing countries to the developed countries and thereby raising the wage of the workers engaged in the concerned production compared to wages of other labour as in Mexico and Chile. It may affect income distribution by raising food prices and thereby hurting the poor landless labourers.

Openness will weaken collective bargaining institutions—as in reality capital mobility shifting from one product to another would be greater than labour mobility. Openness affects economic security—it makes some sectors gain while others lose—Schumpeter's creative destruction gets a booster. There is of course the possibility of reduction of agricultural price fluctuations due to extended trade.

Openness coupled with technological revolutions has made the traded commodities more substitutable than before and therefore the competition is much more intense today. When competition is intense and openness is unavoidable in the context of the present day world economy and international policy, can the World Trade Organization (WTO) mitigate the concomitant hardship to the member-countries, promote well-being at the grassroots level and ensure a bright future for the common people? This is the moot point in any discussion on WTO.

In the developing countries, the grass root consists of the rural poor, small marginal farmers, agricultural labourers, village artisans, shopkeepers and non-agricultural workers. The rural poor depend crucially on local commons such as common environmental resources, forestry, fishery, irrigation, and water grazing lands.

Extreme commercialization in the private hands and extreme nationalization alienate the common people from the community management of the rural resources. Equity and efficiency here go together and redistributive reforms, land distribution and involvement of forestry improve the resource use and is not seriously threatened by globalization.

The new economic policy in the basis of reform has not touched these vital rural resources, which have bearing on the 70 percent of people of our country and other developing countries. Their views on globalization and free trade under the regime of WTO matter much as their reaction has great impact on the governance of the country, which determines the state of things to come through effective implementation of reforms.

In the name of globalization or adherence to the WTO norms, loss of monetary and fiscal options for the nation state and subservience to rules sometimes made by the international trade and financial interests as in Argentina, may spell disaster. Variability in tax-rates exists within states in USA and among other countries. The question is how intelligently you adjust to the rules of the game laid down by the international bodies of which willy nilly you are a member.

For the world as a whole and most essentially the poor-weak countries, the supreme goals of the common future are elimination of poverty, reassertion of sovereignty and world peace. It is often apprehended that submission to the conditions laid down by the world organization would jeopardize sovereignty of the poor countries, aggravate poverty and in the name of greater integration of the countries may help flourish 19th century capitalism and pernicious new imperialism.

Detailed discussion of the implications of the acceptance of the membership of the WTO would dispel the doubts of the people and enable the government to take necessary steps to mitigate the evil effects if any.

A country of the size and importance of India which was a primary member of GATT (now converted in to WTO) since 1947, becoming a member of the WTO is quite natural and desirable. In this state of fait accompli, "the best way to fight fear is to confront it, but at the same time to take prudent and cautious actions".

WTO was born on January 1, 1995 out of GATT on the conclusion of the Uruguay Round of Trade Negotiations. GATT was a loose and provisional organization concerned with trade of only manufactured goods while WTO is based on a sound legal footing spreading its jurisdiction not only over the trade of manufactured goods but also over the trade in services, capital, agricultural products and intellectual property rights (IPRs).

Obviously, the ramification of its regulatory power over almost all important aspects of economic activities is likely to have immeasurable impact on the international economy and the individual economies of the member-countries.

WTO has replaced bilateral trade arrangement by multilateral trade agreement to realize the benefits of free trade in a greater degree and help build up a well-integrated world through unrestricted export-import along with the financial and development aid and co-operation promoted by IMF and the World Bank. WTO has also provided for a quick and legal method of dispute settlement among trading nations.

The impact on grass-root is best manifested by the impact on agriculture. The Agreement on Agriculture (AoA) and trade related investment measures are very much important. The agreement has resulted in reduction of tariff and minimum import access.

The least developed countries have been given certain benefits vis-à-vis agriculture. For example, they do not have to cut domestic support and export subsidies. In turn, the developed countries have wrested some benefits. The so-called Green Box subsidies are allowed which will help economies like the European Union to continue with a major chunk of the subsidization of agriculture. But certain measures included in the so-called Amber Box were allowed.

These measures directly affect trade and production.

Domestic support measures like subsidies, pest control assistance are controlled by the agreement. An aggregate mean use of support (AMS) has been calculated, which would be reduced with economic development.

Some of the rules under WTO provide legitimacy to trade practices which border on criminality including intellectual piracy, MNC derogation of plant breeders' rights by technology, life forms including plants, animals, micro-organisms, genetic material and human life form. Under the Trips Agreement, the provision under GATS provides legitimacy to large scale financial speculative manipulations, privatization of service economy and banking economy which have dismantled welfare state of Europe and North America. Peasant economies have been devastated due to dumping of EU-US grain production and genetically modified seeds. Produce by Cargil and Monsanto have been forced upon farmers, often leading to mass poverty. 30 percent of grain farmers in Western Canada went bankrupt in 1999-2000.

China aware of the consequences said, "A nation cannot develop and become strong without a sense of urgency and a sense of crisis". This implies sacrifice of farmer's interest at the altar of the expanded trade. The unfettered freedom has given much scope to MNCs, which is feared to go a long way to liquidate national enterprises and would destroy people's lives. History does not conclusively prove that a free market system will bring about global prosperity.

Longback, Marx pointed out the propensity of capital to destroy itself. The trinity including WTO, which has paved the way for aggressive capitalism in the garb of openness may be disastrous in the long-run unless there are some counter veiling force.

Speaking of correlation between Keynesianism and viability of capitalism, Galbraith wrote, "The survival of modern market system was in large measure with our achievement. It would not have so survived had it not been for the successful efforts of the social left. Let us not be reticent;

we are the custodians of a political tradition that saved classical capitalism from itself".

Similarly, Hobsbawn observes, "It is one of the ironies of this strange century that the most lasting results of the October Revolution, whose object was the global overthrow of capitalism was to save its antagonist both in war and in peace-by providing it with injunctive to reform itself after Second World War and by establishing the popularity of economic planning furnishing it with some of its procedures for its reform"; capitalism by its very nature is a process of colonization not only of countries but of people.

It breeds over-capacity and the problem of absorption. Same thing has appeared in the international economy at present. The problem of wage fall and reduction of social expenditure shows its ugly head. Neo-capitalism and neo liberalizing does not get rid of Marx's ghost.

The impending danger of unchecked neo-capitalism has to be borne in mind by the developing countries to take precautionary measures as far as possible within the saving clauses of the WTO and other institutions.

Lowering of tariff and dismantling of other restrictions would open up world market whose advantage may be taken by the entrepreneurs. But they are to know quite well wherein their comparative advantage lies.

The developing countries have cost advantages in textiles and agriculture. The developed countries would benefit by opening up service sector and tightening of the intellectual property rights.

In the service sector, the developing countries too benefit by selling their services either as skilled labourer or as high technician-computer engineers of India and China. Migrants from struggling countries in Latin America, South East Asia and other regions are increasingly securing jobs at wages that while low by rich country standards, are far higher than they could dream of back home.

In 2001, workers from low to middle income countries

sent home a staggering US$ 4.3 billion—more than double the level a decade earlier and US$ 5 billion more than that year's official foreign aid to these countries. Labour mobility is bound to be accelerated under WTO regime. Sometimes, of course, developed countries put restriction on migration.

There are certain clauses on labour conditions and wages, which stand on the way of expanded trade of cheap products of the developing countries. They insist on 'fair wage' living wage payment in developing country, otherwise they label the product trade as 'unfair trade'.

To deny trade on these grounds would be to push such a country further into poverty. Same arguments are raised against the export of goods produced by child labour. Rigorous application of the norms laid down by ILO or WTO may worsen the living conditions of the poor in developing countries. These issues are to be considered sympathetically by the developed countries.

The developing countries being member of the international institutions should make honest attempt to gradually remove the practices in production trade that appears to contravene the rules of the game.

For example, with trade liberalization, food prices may go up as a result of more exports. This may harm the interest of the poor consumer while benefiting the farmers. The solution of the problems is not to stop agricultural trade. The problem can be mitigated by targeted public distribution of food or by 'food for work' or public work programmes.

WTO has forced the member countries to reduce tariff. While doing so, it has given some concession to the developing countries. The average reduction of tariff rates offered by developed countries was 38 percent of existing level for imports from all sources taken together. Developing countries offered average tariff reductions of 24 percent.

Duty free and quota free accession to developed markets of the developed world for LDCs will cause problem for India in respect of garments where Bangladesh is competing.

Quantitative restrictions have been abolished. Non-tariff barriers however continue to be used often arbitrarily against exports from developing countries. This issue has to be looked into. Rich nations continue with politics of protectionism, which prevents weaker nations from getting the full benefit of free trade.

How to get at the level playing and induce the rich nations to be genuinely interested in making the world economy a free but just and growing one is the crux of the problem.

No one would dispute the fact that our common future is a happy, stable and prosperous world in which all countries would play their due and get the legitimate share of benefit of free trade. All international institutions have been built with such lofty objectives.

If powerful rich nations manoeuvre to make the institutions dance to their selfish depraved desire tunes, the entire humanity would be in peril. The slowing down of the world economy's progress and continuing poverty and marginalization of the poor, growing unemployment in developed and developing countries despite product expansion bring to the fore the inherent weakness of the free capitalist economy without countervailing force.

In India, rural poverty declined at an annual rate of 2.5 percent during 1970-1980 and at 0.73 percent during the 1990s. Poverty levels declined from 57 percent in 1970s to 33 percent in 1989. On the other hand, urban poverty declined at the rate of 2 percent during 1970-1980 and at 3.05 percent in 1990s. The acceleration in the decline of urban poverty was due to the high income growth achieved during the period of liberalization. The widening rural-urban disparity in incomes is a matter of concern.

The pace of change did not accelerate during the post-reforms period. Total unemployment growth rate declined from 1.57 percent per annum during 1977-87 to 1.45 percent during 1987-99; rural non-agricultural employment growth rate remained around one percent in pre and post-reforms periods (1977-87 and 1987-99). The underlying factors behind this phenomenon and its likely impact on rural economy have not been fully understood.

Nonetheless, it is obvious that liberalization, ushered in by new economic policy of WTO has not met the problem of rural or urban unemployment. Of course, the problem of unemployment has not been so much sharpened by liberalization in our country as in Latin American countries.

Every country tries to secure a condition wherein its export is promoted and imports restricted. This is not possible to achieve. Yet a country like India should determine wherein its commercial interest lies.

Inspection of India's 30 export items for the period 1995-99 indicates only one agricultural item, viz. rice, with a market share of about 6.5 percent in 1999 was affected by protection. Other items like tea, coffee, spices were hardly affected by agricultural protection in developed countries. The dominant export items are cotton textiles, carpets and leather apparel with market share in the range of 12 percent to 30 percent. This defines our interest in both MFA and Social Clause. We are to see what phasing of the MFA would do to industrial tariffs.

The other major export interest for India is export of IT services. These intangible services should be exempt from trade restrictions. Public debate on such issues will enlighten and pressurize the Government to take appropriate steps to secure concessions from WTO.

In conclusion, it may be stated that India needs to expand its external trade, which forms only 0.64 percent of the world trade. Trade is an engine of growth, which could act vigorously only when supplemented by strong domestic policies promoting infrastructure development and productivity efficiency of the export sector.

To take advantage of the changing international environment, a country has to have boldness, clear perspective and determination to sacrifice some at present to gain in future.

It pays to keep in mind what Herman Hesse said, "The values of a future order will be as great as the sacrifice we make today."

11

Poverty, Unemployment and Human Resources Development

The terms poverty, unemployment and development have been variously interpreted in recent years. While pursuing the goal of economic development and enhancement of social welfare, emphasis has been laid on human resource development both as a means and as an end in itself. The concept measurement and methods of eradication of poverty have varied with the state of economy, level of development and outlook on welfare. Unemployment has also been interpreted in different ways viz. principal status, usual status, daily, chronic seasonal etc. Development no longer is understood in terms of Gross National Product (GNP) or per capita income; it has assumed human character and has been treated in terms of Human Development Index (HDI). Of course, in respect of these terms, some ideas have acquired dominance and most of the academic discussions and policy measures have been resorted to in terms of these ideas.

Assuming the dominant meanings of the concepts, let us make an attempt to: (a) highlight the state of poverty, unemployment and human resource development in major Indian States, (b) to ascertain correlation between poverty unemployment and human resource development, and (c) finally to offer suggestive measures for overall development and reduction of inter-state disparity.

Poverty, whether defined in relative or absolute sense, in terms of lack of minimum requirements of calorie intake or lack of entitlement to assets ensuring provision of basic needs (Amartya Sen) is closely linked up with the level and nature of economic development. It is also to be noted that, 'ultimately the process of economic development has to be concerned with what people can or cannot do, e.g. whether they can live long, escape avoidable morbidity, be well-nourished, be able to read and write and communicate, take part in literacy and scientific pursuit and so forth'. [1]

The first Human Development Report, 1990, argued that the real purpose of development should be to enlarge people's choices. By combining indicators of real purchasing power, education and health, the HDI offers a measure of development much more comprehensive than GN alone. In terms of HDI, India ranked 134th place among 173 countries of the world. [2] Human development has been defined by the UNDP as the process of bringing an individual and society to a more organized state wherein the latent or potential in the human being will be realized to a higher degree. The three essentials for this enlarged choice are: (i) a long and healthy life, (ii) acquisition of knowledge, and (iii) access to resources for a decent standard of living.

The above three essentials which constitute Human Development Index (HDI) of UNDP reflect as well as influence economic development. In most cases, poverty and unemployment are offshoots of the absence of human resource development.

It was generally presumed that overall economic development of a country or a region through trickle-down process would bring about economic development of all sections of people and reduce poverty and disparity. But since mid 1960s, thanks to the forceful argument of Late Pakistani economist Mohbul Huq, it has been increasingly realized that income distribution inevitably does not take the route of economic growth, often its trend is reverse.

Hence, UNDP in its report HDR, 1994, has evolved Gender Disparity Adjusted HDI (GDAHDI) on the basis of female-male income ratio and Income Distribution Adjusted HDI (IDAHDI) on the basis of ratio of the income of the lowest income 20 percent of the population to that of the highest earning 20 percent of the population. In 1995, the IMF management noted that equity should be considered not only as an objective of high quality adjustment but also as an instrument of policies to be successful and sustainable. [3] This approach underlines how access to resources for decent standard of living is important for eradication of poverty and unemployment.

It goes without saying that poverty and unemployment which in most cases account for lack of earning are the main cause of illiteracy, ignorance and poor health. Lack of balanced diet coupled with the absence of health awareness cause ill health, morbidity and low longevity. Illiteracy and absence of primary education account for inefficiency in work and weak perception of alternative earning opportunities. Low skill or absence of new skills is also due to absence of elementary and vocational education. Leaving apart slow economic growth, all these explain why poorer sections of the people cannot take advantage of the process of economic development. Hence, the widening of poverty, unemployment and income disparity.

The linkage between human resource development and economic development entailing removal of poverty and unemployment was well realized long back by Indian planners. The First Five Year Plan noted, "Economic planning has to be viewed as an integral part of a wider process aiming not merely at the development of resources in a narrow technical sense but also the development of human faculties and the building up of an institutional framework adequate to the needs and aspirations of the people". [4] However, it may be borne in mind that though there is strong link between economic development and HDI, the relationship is not always one to one. The HDR, 1990, pointed out that income disparity between countries widened while HDI disparity narrowed over years and that there is no close link between economic growth and HDI on an international plane. To have a clear idea on the link between economic development with its distributive aspect and HDI, we shall have to take resort to inter-state study on poverty, unemployment and HDI in regard to our country, India. This is being done in the following section.

Number of studies has been made to highlight the link between human development and economic growth. Bhah, Subha Rao and Kumar have shown that in 1986-87, HDI in India was 0.550 and the coefficient of correlation between HDI and real SDP was 0.714. In India, both trickle-up-effect i.e. economic growth making welfare easier and trickle-down effect, i.e. social development leading to economic growth have operated. In six states, number of poor decreased by 19 percent and in 10 states it increased by 22 percent between 1970 and 1983. In the latter states, the favourable effects and growth and distribution were nullified by population growth. [5]

Education, a significant component of human resource development has the capacity of promoting economic development by creating human capital on a wider scale and enabling various sections of people to earn more. Rightly, Ahluwalia observes, "Unlike physical and financial capital which can expand through accumulation and yet remain highly concentrated in terms of ownership, human capital expansion on any significant scale increasingly involves a wide distribution across population. The dynamics of human capital accumulation, therefore, favours a reduction in inequality". [6] Thus, education entailing larger number of people and skill formation reduces poverty and unemployment.

Education, particularly of females has a bearing on fertility and health of women. High literacy rates in Kerala (87 percent), Tamilnadu (56 percent), Maharashtra (54 percent) of women are found to be associated with low fertility rate (2.2-3.2 children). High fertility rate percentage (4.7 to 5.3) in U.P., M.P., Bihar and Rajasthan are found to be associated with low literacy rates (21 to 28) of women in these states. [7]

A comparison of inter-state variation in per capita income of state domestic product, SDP per capita and that in HDI does not show consistent relation. Chaudhuri, following HDR 1994, calculated HDI of major states and compared it with the SDP/capita of respective states and opined that in respect of HDI-81, Kerala occupied the top position followed by Maharastra and Punjab and the last three positions were occupied by Rajasthan, Bihar and Uttar Pradesh. There was some correlation between HDI and SDP/capita—they are far from identical. For some states (Haryana, Uttar Pradesh and West Bengal), the income rank is significantly ahead of their HDI rank showing that they have potential for translating their incomes into improved well-being of the people. For Kerala and Tamil Nadu, the HDI rank is considerably higher than the income rank, showing that these states have made judicious use of their resources to improve the capabilities and the entitlements of people.

In HDI-91, Kerala, Maharastra and Punjab retained the top three positions while the last three positions were occupied by Madhya Pradesh, Uttar Pradesh and Bihar. The degree of correlation was .585. For states such as Haryana, Karnataka Punjab and West Bengal, the SDP/capita rank was significantly higher than the HDI rank, showing that these states have the potential to improve human development. For Kerala and Tamilnadu, the HDI rank was ahead of their income rank, showing that these states have made more efficient and judicious use of their resources. [8]

If we compare HDI-91 rank with rural poverty of states for 1993-94, we do not find any consistent correlation. In HDI-91, Bihar, Uttar Pradesh and Madhya Pradesh have the lowest ranks in that order, but in respect of rural poverty, though Bihar has the highest poverty ratio, Madhya Pradesh and Uttar Pradesh have the low poverty ratios. In these two states, poverty does not appear to be a major cause of low HDI. Kerala occupies first position in HDI-91 but in respect of poverty it is not the least poor state. West Bengal is the second least poor (rural) State, but in HDI its rank is 8th. Thus, it appears that though HDI may contribute to eradication of poverty to certain extent, it cannot be a sole factor for poverty alleviation.

Further, between 14 states, disparity in poverty ratios was seen to increase over 1977-78 and 1993-94 both in rural and urban sectors. Gujrat and Tamilnadu experienced faster decline in poverty ratio than the national average. In Assam, Bihar and Punjab, poverty ratio increased in the post-1987-88 period. Inter-state disparity in average consumption in rural sector increased between 1987-88 and 1993-94. Divergence between 15 states in terms of per capita product also increased in this period. [9] This is not the case in regard to HDI, Chaudhuri (1997) found that coefficient of variation of the HDI values of states for 1981 was .183 and that for 1991 was .171.

This indicates that the level of human development was more equitable in 1991. Since no region has a perfect income distribution, the Income Distribution Adjusted HDI gives a drastically changed ranking of States. Maharashtra occupies the topmost position followed by West Bengal and Andhra Pradesh. [10] A comparison of the poverty levels and educational achievements of say Kerala and Uttar Pradesh also defies the claim that it is poverty that prevents the poor from sending their children to school. In 1987-88, there was not much difference between Kerala and U.P. in respect of poverty level (44 and 42 percent) but there was great difference in literacy level (90 percent) in Kerala and 40.5 percent in U.P. [11]

As there is no consistent correlation between poverty, income per capita and HDI, so also there is no consistent correlation between HDI and unemployment. It is found that Bihar where literacy and HDI level was very low, the unemployment level was also very low at 12 to 16 per 1000 persons for male. Kerala having top-most position in HDI had the highest unemployment rate of 57 to 63 per 1000 persons. Rajasthan and Orissa which have low HDI rank have also low unemployment rate. It would be absurd to infer from the data that high HDI causes high unemployment and low HDI accounts for low unemployment. Unemployment has to be explained by other factors than HDI.

The preceding analysis shows that though there is some link between poverty, unemployment and HDI, the relationship is not always consistent and strong. The study on inter-state disparity shows that always the lowest positions in the matters of HDI, employment and income/consumption are occupied by states like Bihar, Uttar Pradesh, Rajasthan and Orissa. States like Kerala, Maharashtra and Punjab occupy the top positions.

If human beings are the subject of our concern, the experiences of the advanced states like Kerala, Maharashtra and Punjab suggest that in the realm of planning, emphasis should be laid on development of education, health, agriculture and other poverty alleviation measures like rural industrialization and generation of self-employment which would go a long way in enhancing individuals, capabilities and entitlement.

Further, the perpetuating low positions of Bihar, Madhya Pradesh and Orissa may be attributed to the existence of a substantial percentage of Scheduled Caste and Scheduled Tribe and other disadvantaged population in the States. Special attention may be paid to the specific problems of these weaker sections and appropriate measures may be undertaken with earnestness to improve their conditions in all respects.

Cultural and psychological constraints may be responsible for the low HDI particularly, Gender Distribution Adjusted HDI in U.P. and Rajasthan along with M.P., Bihar and Orissa. Here, creation of awareness and motivation will be a catalytic factor for change.

Since there is a strong relation between growth and poverty and positive relation between growth and inequality one has to make a Hobson's choice between growth and inequality. Growth cannot be sacrificed for the sake of equality, though corrective measures by the state are desirable to check growing inequality. Growth with equity is no doubt an optimal combination for generating good macro-conditions needed to achieve human development objectives. As Keynes observed in General Theory, "Soon or late it is ideas, not vested interests, which are dangerous for good or evil". In the context of India, new ideas of development are called for. Social scientists are to integrate human development issues into development planning.

There is unequal distribution of education in India. Its education gini coefficient was amongst the highest in the world (0.74 in 1990). Improvements in education investment that focus on gender equality, distribution and quality can yield high social and economic returns.

End Notes

1. Sen, Amartya (1984), Resources, Values and Development, pp. 496-549.
2. UNDP (1993), Human Development Report, pp 9-17.
3. Sengupta, Arjun (1998), Equity for Growth: An IMF Prescription Worth Following, Times of India, 9th July.
4. Bhah, K., Subha Rao, A. and Kumar Jayat, "Human Development and Economic Growth" in Special Issue on Human Development, Margin, Vol. 25, No. 2, Part-II.
5. Ahluwalia, M.S. (1990), Policies for Poverty Alleviation, Asian Development Review, 8 (I), pp. 111-112.
6. Singh, R.R., Education of Adolscent Girls, Margin, Vol. 25, Part II, January-March 1993.
7. Chaudhuri, Saumya, Regional Disparities in Human Development in India, Paper presented in Seminar on Regional Studies at Jodhpur University.
8. Gupta, S.P. (1998), Post Reform India-Emerging Trends, Allied Publishers, pp. 203-206.
9. Choudhuri, Sauma Opcit.
10. Bhatty, Kiran, Educational Deprivation in India: A Survey of Field Investigation, EPW, July 4-10, 1998, p. 173.
11. Narayan, K.R. (1993), For a New Strategy of Development, Margin, January-March 1993.

12

Agriculture in Developing Countries

Agriculture holds key to economic development in many developing countries of the world. Globalization and the WTO have brought countries of the world much closer and forced them to be competitive in their economic activities. Prior to WTO, agriculture in developing countries was more or less isolated and relatively free from the influence of the developed countries. Now, the agriculture of the developing countries like India faces new problems and challenges in a free international regime. The problems or issues that need serious consideration relate to:

1. Production and productivity of agriculture.
2. Pattern of production with a view to meeting the requirements of the people, economic growth and expansion of foreign trade—which calls for diversification of agriculture.
3. Cost of production and technology needed.
4. Sustainability of development—ecological issues.
5. Rural employment and seasonality of agriculture.
6. Linkage between agriculture and industry.
7. Reforms in planning and investment—Re-fixation of priority.
8. New look at agrarian reforms.
9. Poverty, malnutrition and empowerment.

The issues to be tackled require not only enlightened and efficient administration but also people's support and active participation and sympathetic attitude of other countries, international organizations and their assistance.

Interest in sustainable development and reduction of poverty has grown along with the spread of globalization. In September 2000, 147 heads of States and representative of 189 nations committed themselves to freeing the human race from want and hunger. They endorsed Millennium Development Goal (MDGs). The Delhi Sustainable Development Summit 2001, debated issues on sustainable development. The world Summit on Sustainable Development (WSSD) held in Johannesburg in 2002, advanced the concept of partnership between different stake holders. The president of the World Business Councils for Sustainable Development, Bjom Stigson observes, "business cannot succeed in a society that falls".

The Living Planet Report brought out by WWF revealed that between 1970 and 2000, LPI has declined by 40 percent i.e. population of wild species has declined by 40 percent. The second report Humanity's Ecological Footprint (HEF) that measures environmental sustainability and assesses humanity's demand for earth's renewable natural resources shows that HEF has grown to exceed the earth's biological carrying capacity by 20 percent. The reduction of living species and overuse of the world's natural resources is clearly not a sustainable strategy for humanity. Coordinated efforts both of industrial and agricultural sector is needed for sustaining ecology. In agricultural sector, particular development of bio-technology and genetic engineering is essential to spare the environment from various types of pollution afflicting land and water, food and life.

In most of the developing countries, majority of people live in rural areas and depend on agriculture. Globalisation has hard hit the poor and marginalized people living in rural areas. Professor Josef Stiglitz has pointed out that globalization has benefited the richer sections of the people, not the poor.

The share in developing countries of the population living below poverty line has declined from 28 to 24 percent but the number of poor people has increased marginally. In South Asia and Sub-saharan Africa, the increase was substantial between 1987-1998. Poor in South Asia and Sub-saharan Africa constitute 70 percent of the poor and their number increased by 19 percent during the above period. There are regional variations in changes in poverty ratio. Out of seven African countries, poverty in 4 countries including Nigeria, Zambia and Zimbabwe increased. In Latin America, poverty fell in Brazil and Chile but rose in Mexico and Venezuela. In Asia, there was reduction of poverty in Bangladesh but no change in Pakistan and Sri Lanka. In India, poverty came down from 36 percent in 1993-94 to 26 percent in 1999-2000. The data is disputed. Wide variation of poverty exists in our country. States like Orissa, Bihar, U.P., Assam, Maharastra and West Bengal have high levels of poverty. In most states, it is the poor agricultural performance that accounts for perpetual poverty.

Regression analysis shows that non-farm employment growth, increase in agricultural prosperity and diversification of agriculture reduces poverty (P.K. Pal, India Economic Association, 86th Conference Volume).

Land reforms which have been implemented half-heartedly have to be done sincerely and effectively. Tenants are to be given real security and incentive to raise productivity. The experience of Japan and Korea shows that there is no contradiction between land reform and dynamies of development. The land reforms must be linked by institutional reforms which may provide tenure security, adequate assistance by way of credit, technological know how and creating proper distributive channel (Jagdish Prasad, Journal of Social and Economic Studies, Vol. XVI, A.N. Sinha Institute of Social Studies).

70 percent of the poor in our country is accounted for by U.P., M.P., Bihar, Maharastra, West Bengal and Orissa. 48 percent of the poor belong to agricultural sector and 28 percent self-employment in agriculture. Area cultivated by small and marginal farmers increased from 29 percent to 36 percent of the total between 1985-86 and 1995-96. During the last 25 years area under food grain production has declined by 10 percent. The land vacated by cereals has been occupied by oilseeds, cotton, tobacco and sugarcane.

Still then, cereal accounts for 64.30 percent of cultivated land. There has been increased use of modern inputs and increasing free trade. During 1993-94 to 1999-2000, value of agricultural output increased from ₹ 2,04,874 crore to ₹ 4,05,378 crore and value of input from ₹ 55401 crore to ₹ 1,03,555 crore. Agricultural growth rate declined from 3.8 percent per annum in 1980s to 2.4 percent per annum in 1990s. There has been deceleration in productivity growth of all crops. In sugarcane the productivity growth rate was less than I.P.C. and in tobacco and cotton it was negative in 1990s. As a result, the terms of trade (index of prices received divided by index of prices paid) remained around 103-105 in contrast to the rising trend in the previous decades.

Policies adopted to save the vulnerable sections have not been very much successful. The institutions of extension service and credit have failed. The role of extension institutions in acting as a conduit between the scientists and users is practically non-existent. The rural financial institutions are not advancing credit with the larger use of purchased inputs. The reasons advanced are: (i) less absorptive capacity in rural areas, and (ii) high transaction costs and greater risks.

Measures to raise productivity in dry areas and dairy sector should be given priority. Investment in strengthening land and water resources has declined since 1980s. 42 percent of the geographical area of the country comprises degraded land. Supportive institutions are to be built up and activised. 8 million SHGs should be used to help the vulnerable sections of the farmers.

Capital Formation in Agriculture

Private gross fixed capital formation (GFCF) as percentage of GDP in agriculture rose from 3.64 percent in 1975-79 to 4.89 in 2000-02. Public GFCF declined during the period from 3.95 to 1.54. GFCF overall declined from 7.54 to 6.43 percent. Credit rose from 8.55 percent to 15.89 percent and subsidies rose from 2.58 percent to 6.05 percent. Revenue receipts from agriculture declined from 6.27 percent to 1.15 percent between 1975-79 and 2000-02.

At 1993-94 prices, public investment which was ₹ 5,986 crore in second half of 1970s rose to ₹ 7,300 crore in early 1980s and then declined. The rate of return to private capital stock was 19.42 percent in 1970s and now stands at 6.6 percent.

It is estimated that an increase in net sown area of one hectare increases agricultural output by ₹ 22,284 at 1993-94 prices. An increase of IPC terms of trade raises agricultural output by ₹ 1,118 crore. An increase in subsidy of ₹ 1 increases GDP in agriculture by ₹ 3.19, ₹ 1 increase in capital stock raises ₹ 35.21 over a life span of 58 years.

It is found that 1 percent shift of resources from subsidy to public investment would raise GDPA by 1.82 to 2.73 percent in the long run. So, from long-term point of view, diversion from subsidy to capital formation is desirable. (Ramesh Chand and Pramod Kumar, EPW, December 25; 31, 2004)

Labour Force and the Poor

Between 1993-94 and 1999-2000, in India, the number of working poor declined from 114.8 million to 102.3 million i.e. by 12.6 million. The rural share declined from 81.8 to 80 percent. Unemployed in rural India increased from 35,41,000 to 46,93,000. In urban India, it increased from 38,70,000 to 47,32,000. Only 3 percent of the rural working poor received regular wages compared to 8 percent for non-poor in 1993-94; same was in 1999-2000 for rural worker getting regular wages.

The World Employment Report, 1998-99, says that since 1970, unemployment in developed countries has increased twice. World Investment Report points out that unemployment would go on increasing due to modern technology. ILO Report 2000, points to the widening disparity between the rich and poor. According to Ethan B. Capstein, the hourly wage of the unskilled worker has decreased by 27 percent between 1973 and 1997 in Europe and America.

Migration of labour from developing countries creates unemployment in developed countries too. Three million workers reached US from other countries in 1994. US's free trade created 2 lakh jobs in China. In India, between 1993-94 and 2000-01, the percentage of poor agricultural labour of the total labour force from 41 to 47 percent. The percentage of agricultural labour increased from 28 to 31 percentage in our country.

Mckinsey and Co. estimated that MNCs spent about US$ 35 billion in 2002 on import of service from other countries and this will increase by 30-40 percent per annum till 2008. Business Week reported that exports of IT etc. will create 4 million jobs in India by 2003.

Exports and Investment

Since 1993-94 till 1995-96, our exports increased by 20 percent per annum after which it declined for few years. However, in 2001 it increased by 20 percent. Along with exports, imports also rose. That is why net trade deficit continues and is now 4 percent of GDP. Foreign direct investment (FDI) in India is only 1.6 percent of its GDP, whereas it is 5 percent of their GDPs in China and Brazil. We are to take more effective steps to increase exports and decrease imports and attract more foreign direct investment in desirable sectors. Cumulative amount of FDI inflows in the country from April 2000 to December 2012 stood at US$ 2,80,412 million. Herein comes the importance of agricultural development with specific purpose of providing export and development of agro industries processing and packing of agricultural products.

350 MNCs controlled 30 percent of world trade in 1970s. Now they control 45 percent. In 1991-92, export of agro-product was 14.4 percent of the total export, it came down to 13.3 percent in 1994-95. Subsidy to agriculture was reduced by 20 percent. According to Jagdish Bhagwati, structural adjustment did not produce desirable result in 1990s in India as

proper attention was not given to agriculture and education.

There is vast potential for growth in 20 industries in our country which comprise food, clothing, jute, paper, leather, chemical, steel and metal industries. In 1990s, employment in these industries increased at the rate of 2.9 percent per annum. Production increased at the rate of 9.1 percent per annum against 7.1 percent increase in 1980s. Compound annual growth rate in agriculture in 1993-2002 was 0.9 percent in Orissa, 1.2 percent in Bihar, 4.2 percent in West Bengal and 3.0 percent in Andhra Pradesh.

Subsidy: A Knotty Issue

Developed countries under WTO force the developing countries to reduce their direct subsidy to agriculture and its export. But EU gives direct ₹ 8,800 crore and US ₹ 5,400 crore annually as subsidy to agriculture.

US gives subsidy to 22,500 affluent farmers and causes distress for the 10 million African farmers. Major portion of this subsidy goes to food and soybean. EU gives 2 dollar subsidy a day to the farmers. During 1995-99, EU and US increased their subsidy to farmers by 30 percent.

US gives ₹ 300 crore subsidy to cotton growers annually and it reduces cotton price by 10 to 20 percent. As a result, West Africa loses US$ 250 million per annum. EU gives 100 billion subsidies to sugar and brings down sugar price.

Japan gives help to the rice growers to the extent of 6 times the production cost. The subsidy given by OCED Countries is six times the aid to developing countries. Is there any justification to force developing countries to reduce subsidy?

Employment in agriculture in our country rose by 1.5 percent per annum during 1983-1994. The elasticity of employment to the economic growth was 0.4 percent in 1983-94 and it came down to 0.15 in 1994-2000.

During the last 5 years, expenditure on agriculture has come down from 4.9 percent to 2.6 percent of budget expenditure. Expenditure on rural development has come down from 14.5 percent to 6 percent.

In 1995-96, in India, fertilizer subsidy was ₹ 5,400 crore, food subsidy ₹ 5,250 thousand crore and export subsidy ₹ 3,150 crore.

Vegetable and horticulture export of India forms 8 percent of the total world export. There is ample scope for expanding its export. Globalization by forcing us to reduce agricultural subsidy and open the market for the world, brings in some hurdles and offers some opportunity.

To check the evil effects of globalization and reap its benefits the followings steps should be taken.

1. Infrastructure of the economy—road communication, electricity education and administration has to be strengthened.
2. Foreign direct investment has to be channelised into sectors and areas that would benefit the economy most.
3. Massive social work-public work programme has to be taken to help growth of employment and provide security to the workers, particularly rural workers.
4. Crop insurance and unemployment insurance are to be implemented to meet agricultural fluctuation situation and reduce suffering of the poor.
5. Stress has to be given on increase in production and productivity of agriculture and developing agro-industries.
6. Expansion of export of food articles, garments, leather and jewellery works to be stepped up.
7. Institution of creditable risk mitigating measures.
8. Investment for strengthening land and water resources.
9. Strengthening supportive institutions for extension service and credit distribution.
10. G-60 countries should pressurize WTO to ask EU and US to reduce their subsidy and waive out stringent stipulations for developing countries on the plea of free-trade and ethical norms for labour.

13

Globalization and Cultural Relations

Since 1980, the world has experienced unprecedented changes. There have taken place the unexpected collapse of the Soviet Union accelerating the decline of the sway of socialism and expediting the tide of capitalism, spectacular growth of information technology bringing the distant lands closer on air, swift moves and counter moves of ideas creating feelings, sweet and sour.

Whatever might have been the drawbacks of communist rule, it solidly stood against imperialism and opposed the grabbing appetite of capitalism; the overwhelming ideas of equity, equality, fraternity and secularism checked the pernicious tendency of religious fundamentalism. With neo-imperialism and financial capitalism riding on the wave of quick enrichment of the wise and privileged upper and middle class, obnoxious display of selfishness and consumerism came to surface. Linked with it fatalism, faith in ritualistic religion, attempt to divert the mind of the poor from rationality whatever is there to the glamour of the coming days, raise their ugly heads. Either as an accompaniment or as a violent reaction, terrorism of various colours and religious fundamentalism appear in various parts of the developing countries. Rudderless capitalism has brought in its train many an evil which cover up some good impacts it makes.

It was hoped, with US becoming the super power without any formidable challenge as in the past from the USSR, there would be no need of atomic weapons. But the terrorist attack on the World Trade Centre in New York on September 11, 2001 belied this hope. The sudden attack by Laden, on the heart of the world finance has unnerved all states of the world and put social and political thinkers to deep brooding. The former chief of the CIA has said, "We are deeply disturbed confronting a world fraught with most uncertain quick and critical conflict".

A revolutionary change has occurred in the international system. The concept of nation-state has changed. In about one third of the member countries of the UN there has appeared ethnic conflict and revolt. National boundary has become indistinct. Free movement of drugs and weapons has helped the terrorists. Enormous financial flow has disrupted banking business and weakened the sovereignty of the states. The disturbing situation has given rise to an entity which is called the post-national state.

Many social scientists think that the concept of nation state is now losing its hold. Francis Fukuyama in his book 'The End of History and the Last Man' observes that the fight between democracy and totalitarianism is over. Totalitarianism has come to an end. There would be not conflict in developed states but in the developing Third World. There may be some fear of war as they are still steeped in the quagmire of ideological conflict. Fukuyama may be correct for the developed countries but not for the developing ones because totalitarianism does not mean only communism, nor democracy is the only alternative to totalitarianism. There are other types of authoritarianism in the world like ethnic nationalism and religions fundamentalism. Hence, there is no possibility of the end of ideological or physical conflict.

Samuel Huttington in his thought provoking book, 'The Clash of Civilizations' has raised another issue, when he says, "There would be clash of civilizations not due to economic or ideological cause, it would take place due to cultural differences. The nation-state would lead the conflict. In international politics, conflict between various ethnic groups and cultures will be a knotty issue".

The conflict between one civilization and another is not only real but also fundamental. The gap due to distance is being obliterated by social change and economic modernization. But cultural difference is not easily washed away. It is very difficult to remove cultural difference. Alvin and H.B. Toffler in their new book, "War and Antiwar" observed, "We believe there would be conflict between cultures in future. But this won't happen on Huntington's line basing on caste and religion. It will occur between highly industrialized cultures".

According to Toffler, the first wave of civilization was agricultural, the second industrial and the third is globalization. In his view, countries of the world are situated in three phases, and huge bloodshed would occur due to conflict between civilizations. To refute the views of Toffler and Huntington, Eisuke Sakakibera in his essays, "The End of Progressivism" says, the Cold War happened due to classical capitalism. There is not conflict alone; there has been co-existence and cooperation of civilizations. Conflict is not inevitable due to existence of different civilizations. It was due to the reaction of these civilizations to western theory of progress.

Globalization is now at an infant stage. Many are of view that even though nation state has played a major role in international field in last 200 years, the influence of major civilizations is greater. According to Dipankar Benerjee, the role of nation state won't be minor in future. The theory of conflict based on civilization gap may appear fine, yet it cannot explain all tussles of the world.

History will not come to an end; co-existence of civilization would remain. The recent happening points to the conflict between terrorists and the nation state in some cases, trade war between nation states in others.

Environmental issues are becoming important, conflict between civilizations may be bitter due to lack of liberal attitude and tolerance. If the developed world converts the third world into neo-colonies by applying weapons of modernization, this will create conflict and rivalry in the world. If we can use modernization as a weapon of understanding and goodwill looking at the background of history and culture, it would have salubrious effects. It is difficult to predict the future change.

History proves, whether the world is unipolar or bipolar, it is autocratic behaviours of powerful states which breed enmity among nations causing war-crisis. It is true that after WW II, the opportunistic exploitative policy of US has generated hatred and rivalry among nations and sowed the seed of terrorism. The rise and fall of Taliban and partiality of US towards Palestine stand testimony to it.

There are two types of terrorism in the world, one is created by state and other is created by the anti-state power. Terrorism is nothing but an effort to realize religious or ideological goal with means of force, threat and violence. "Terrorism as everyone knows thrives in societies where there is no public space for people to vent their grievances and where no political mechanism exists for those grievances to be addressed". (Reza Aslan, Tactics in Economic War, Statesman, 26 April, 2009)

Whatever ideal may mould the structure of the society, at the roots is the power mechanism. The state may wield terrorist weapons in name of the people's welfare. Under the veils of democracy the State may encroach upon human rights. The so-called secular state may harass the minority on the plea that the majority view constitutes democracy. We consider it legal when states fight for political and religious purposes. It is characterized as guerrilla warfare. But when it is on the common people, it is termed terrorism. Terrorists may join together to fight against oppression and exploitation, but this will kill humanity and cripple man by distrust and hatred.

Sauder and Chaumsky say, "the dividing lines between man and man are power of judgment on the one hand and religion and ethnic attachment on the other. Thinner the judging power, stronger is group rivalry".

Use of violence, whether by state or civil organization creates crisis exploitation of the poor by capitalists' power, unethical attitude of the state for retaining power, extreme and violent methods adopted for the purpose will spell disaster. The process of the present globalization with capitalistic avarice may ignite destruction. But, it is not inevitable and uncheckable. Perception of imminent danger has moved the nation states and international organizations to think of corrective measures.

Knowledge, Compassion and Cooperation

A German philosopher, once observed that knowledge without compassion prods to act as a Satan in the Bible. The onward march of science and technology cannot be halted. The world cannot be pushed back to the hoary past. The future can and must be brightened for the survival of the humanity. Systematic efforts have commenced to fight the serious dangers facing the world—ecological imbalances and terrorism. The other day during his historic address to the Turkish Parliament, President Barak Obama reached out to the Muslim world by stating, "the United States is not and will never be at war with Islam". This mind-set of the president of the most powerful state of the world would definitely influence the Islamic world. Amidst spontaneous cheer a college student from Syria with emotion said to Reza Aslan, "with these words Obama just wiped away the stain of the past eight years".

Globalization with rapidly rising money power of the multinational corporations may create some economic problems in the Third World, but by facilitating easy exchange of views, intermixture of arts, literature and culture, it may prevent the hegemony of one or two cultures, it might effect a happy blending of different cultures, in the process of give and take enrich all cultures and mollify the conflict between civilizations. Influence of a culture on the other is transmitted through language English at present is the dominant international language. Many feel that the erstwhile colonies may be adversely affected. But Huntington observed that with the setting up of democratic societies, indigenous languages would prevail upon the English language in non-western societies. Sanjukta Dasgupta thinks, different nations being alien to each other in terms of languages, religion, skin colour and social origin, cultural negation could only happen on intellectual level—socially and emotionally the divide would be too difficult to bridge.

Karl Marx and Engels long back observed that perusal of world literature would aid in redefining cultural boundaries and borders. They wrote, "The intellectual creation of individual nations become common property. National one-sidedness and narrow-mindedness become more and more impossible and from the numerous national and local literatures there arises a world literature (Indian Literature, 248, p. 236). The observation regarding literature is also appropriate to culture and civilizations. Intermingling of cultures would promote co-existence of different civilizations, retaining their separate uniqueness.

With the democratic process having sway over political set up of major countries and international problems like ecological disturbance and terrorism posing great danger, surely there would be serious efforts to keep the evil consequences of globalization at bay.

14

TRIPS and its Impact on Indian Pharmaceutical Sector

An important area of agreement among the members of the WTO refers to Trade Related Intellectual Property Rights (TRIPS). This agreement compels the member countries to follow uniform policy regarding the use of the rights on intellectual property earned. Intellectual property rights may cover many items, of which pharmaceutical sector is very important in view of its impact on common people.

Here a humble attempt is made: (a) to analyse the contents of the TRIPS in relation to pharmaceutical sector, (b) to review the erstwhile Indian patent rights, and (c) to examine the impact of the new patent law in WTO regime on the Indian pharmaceutical industry and the consumers.

Trade Related Intellectual Property Rights (TRIPS) means rights granted to the creators of innovative work in relation to trade. The unauthorized use of intellectual property is an infringement of the right of the owner. Intellectual property right includes patent, copy right, trademark, industrial design, geographical indications, trade secrets and layout designs of integrated circuits. In the field of trade, patent assumes great significance; patents provide property rights to inventions. The TRIPS Agreement provides that an invention to be registered as a patent, it must be new, involves an inventive step and be capable of industrial application. The Agreement further stipulates that countries shall grant patents for inventions in all fields of technology and for both products and processes, including those used in manufacturing the process. The product/processes which countries are permitted to exclude from patent ability are diagnostic, therapeutic and surgical methods for treatment of humans and animals, plants and animals other than micro-organisms, essentially biological process for the production of plants and animals other than non-biological and microbiological processes.

Under the TRIPS arrangement of WTO, patent right can be granted to the foreigners irrespective of the place of invention, sector of the technology and the product—"patent rights be available for any invention whether products or processes, patent rights enjoyable without discrimination as to the place of invention, the field of technology and whether products are all imported or locally produced". For free and unfettered trade, a uniform patent law shall operate all over the world as per the WTO stipulation from 2005. The developing countries as members of the WTO were asked to amend their patent law gradually between 1995 and 2005. Accordingly, the Government of India introduced a Bill to amend the existing patent law in the Parliament in 1995 which could not be passed due to vehement opposition. Ultimately, the amended Bill was passed and the Patents Act, 1970 was amended in 2002.

The cosmetic treatment incorporated in the Patent Amendment Act, 2002 following the direction of the WTO panel to India was triggered by a complaint filled by the US. The major changes focusing on the pharmaceutical sector were in the areas of redefining patentable inventions, granting new rights, extension of the term of protection uniformly for 20 years, providing the onus of proof on the violation case of infringement, conditions for compulsory licences and creation of an appellate board. All these changes unfortunately did not address the ground realities bedevilling the industrial manufacturing sector in India. 'Novelty', 'Inventive step' and 'Industrial application' are the three tests for use of patent. Utility model could have been incorporated for acquiring industrial property protection as in Korea and Japan. (J. George, Patent (Amendment) Act, 2002 and Technological Innovation, EPW, February 26, 2005)

Ministers conference of 2001 (Doha Declaration) stated, "The TRIPS Agreement does not and cannot prevent members from taking measures to protect public health. TRIPS Agreement states that intellectual property rights and enforcement of intellectual property rights should among other things, "be conducive to social and economic welfare and to a balance of rights and obligations". Doha Declaration further stated that every WTO member has 'the right to grant compulsory licences and freedom to determine the ground upon which such licenses are granted'. This acknowledges the fact that the future of drug industry in a country like India hinges on the ability of the producers to licence out technologies from the owners of proprietary technologies.

India has to guard against ever greening of pharmaceutical patents of the Incrementally Modified Drugs (IMDS) which in 85 percent of the cases do not provide significant improvement over currently marketed therapies and only helps raise prices. Between 1994 and 2003, about 9000 product patent applications have been put in mail box which are to be screened to eliminate IMDS. In TRIPS Agreement, 'novelty', 'inventive step' and 'industrial application', the three criteria for issue of patent are not clearly defined. Hence, the royalty from the drug producer to the generic producer to the patenter, has to be properly determined. India is the only country where post-grant opposition to issue of patent is allowed, it has put patent application in a disadvantageous position. The post-grant opposition should be dispensed of with. (Biswajit Dhar, Niranjan Rao, Reflections on a TRIPS Complaint Law, EPW, April 9, 2005)

The TRIPS provided three deadlines for India to comply with the multilateral patent regime. The first deadline was in 1995 to introduce mailbox protection and exclusive marketing rights (EMRS). The second was in 2000 to comply with TRIPS provision on duration of present protection. India amended the Patents Act, 1999 and 2002 well beyond the WTO's required lines. The third and final deadline was to introduce product patent protection for pharmaceuticals and agrochemicals by January 2005. To meet the deadline, the government issued an ordinance on December 26, 2004, to amend its Patents Act, 1970. The ordinance incorporated 74 amendments and took it beyond the TRIPS requirement. The amendments took India into TRIPS plus regime. These amendments invited protest from multilateral organizations like WTO and UNAIB who described it as potentially devastating to developing and least developed countries who are dependent on Indian generic drugs.

The Government redrafted the Bill and sent to the Parliament which was finally voted in Rajya Sabha on March 23. The key amendments which could have lasting effects on LDCs refer to the scope of patentability, immunity to generic manufacturers, pre-grant opposition, compulsory licence provisions and licence for export. Some of the amendments are still riddled with loopholes and ambiguities.

The Indian Patent Act, 1970 limited the scope of patentability by defining the term invention patents, inventive step and industrial application. The 2005 Bill however introduced three new definitions viz. inventive step, new invention and pharmaceutical substance. These definitions are extremely ambiguous with numerous technical loopholes that will facilitate ever greening of patents. A feature of invention is said to be having economic significance which would broaden the scope for patents. The term pharmaceutical substance in place of new chemical entity also broadens the scope for patent.

The terms significant investment and reasonable royalty would create litigation between generic manufactures and patent holders. The compulsory licence provision also does not exploit flexibility within TRIPS. The procedure to obtain compulsory licence appears to be cumbersome. The legislature has chosen not to incorporate the flexibilities that are available within TRIPS to safeguard public interest. (K. M. Gopa Kumar and Tahir Amin, Patents (Amendment) Bill, 2005-A Critique, EPW, April 9, 2005)

Implications of IPRs and the New Patent Rights

The TRIPS Agreement essentially mandates the protection of intellectual property, which is increasingly becoming an integral part of technology transfer and license agreements in the context of a liberalized economy.

The Indian Patent Act, 1970 is criticized as being detrimental to free flow of trade into the country. This is so because the Act gives special rights to the producer for the distinct process of production, not for the product. As a result, a product having similar quality can be produced by different processes. For example, an Indian company can produce Felodipin, a substitute of Amlod pin, a drug for heart disease and sell at a cheaper price. This cannot be done if the patent law covers both the products and processes. In Indian Patent Act, 1970, there was no provision for issuing patent for food or agricultural product. The scope of the new Patent Act, 2005 is wider.

Prior to the enactment of the Indian Patent Act, 1970, the foreign companies were selling their antibiotic medicines at an exorbitantly high rate in India and other developing countries as stated by the Kefaver Committee of USA. Hathi Committee in 1975 observed that by 1970s, the MNCs were controlling about 70 percent of the Indian drug market. 1970 Patent Act brought about a change in this situation. As acknowledged in the 1980 Unidor Conference, the Indian companies produced 70 percent of the total drugs consumed in India. This was possible due to: (a) establishment of public enterprises like India Drug and Pharmaceutical Ltd. in the field of medicine production, (b) issue of license for all sorts of drug production with great privilege to the Indian companies, (c) regulation of drug price since 1950, and (d) Indian Patent Act (IPA), 1970.

Because of the above acts, the foreign companies were forced to reduce their drug price and establish their own industries in India. In 1987, Rajiv Gandhi narrowed the area of regulation of drugs and the process culminated in the latest amendment of the Act in 2005.

Against the formidable will of US upholding the interest of the MNCs, India managed to push a set of flexibilities into the Uruguay Round Agreement on Trade Related Aspects of Intellectual Property Rights that could be used to protect the consumers against those of the multinationals. But ultimately, as the Patent (Amendment) Ordinance, 2004 evened, the government catapulted to pharmaceutical multinationals, foreign and domestic. The Ordinance failed in the area of compulsory licensing.

The TRIPS Agreement allows countries to issue compulsory licenses for the manufacture of patented drugs without the patent holders' permission in case of public health emergencies. It also gives the country the sole right to determine if a particular situation represents a public health emergency. The Ordinance took no advantage of this provision. Instead, it retained the old provision for issue of compulsory licence. Under this, the Controller of Patents must take into account such matters as the time elapsed since the issuance of the patent efforts made by the patentee to make full use of invention and the ability of the applicant for the compulsory license to work the invention to the public advantage. This would delay the issuance of licence and give scopes to protest. Under TRIPS Agreement, it would be perfectly legitimate to issue compulsory licence expeditiously, postponing any representation against it.

The Ordinance provides for compulsory licence for export of generic versions of patent drugs to Third World countries that lack the capacity to produce but gives the Controller of Patents the power to specify any criteria that he sees fit. Such blanket bureaucratic discretion can only delay the beginning of production and export of drugs. The WTO decision of August 30, 2003 provides straight forward conditions and there is no rationale for India to go further by placing additional conditions on the licence.

The export of generic drugs by the Indian firms have been responsible for bringing the prices of anti-retroviral therapy from US$ 12,000 to US$ 140 per year and the value of such restraints on drug prices to the world's poor can be scarcely underestimated. [1]

Further, the 20 years patent required under TRIPS Agreement is already excessively long and there should be no room for extension under any circumstances. The weakening of the provisions for pre-grant opposition to patent applications is not desirable. The TRIPS Agreement imposes no such requirement. Canada and the UK which give priority to public interest have much tougher pre-grant opposition provisions.

IPA, 1970 provided basis for balancing the act between national interests and global commitments. TRIPS obligations are heavily biased towards protecting pharmaceutical industry. IPA, 1970 had two dominant objectives—to develop a prosperous indigenous pharmaceutical industry and to provide low-cost access to medicines for the Indian population. Thanks to the Act, by 2004, many Indian firms have become leading players in international market. The new Act is in tune with TRIPS and the patents are issued for 20 years.

The small and medium sized firms perfected the act of reverse engineering under IPA, 1970. In the new Act, patentable subject matter is not clearly spelt out. What constitutes new chemical entity and new medical entity are not clearly defined. This gives scope for legal interpretation which would serve the interests of the big players not of the country.

Three vital steps are necessary for a patent, namely, uniqueness, inventive step and capable of industrial use. To what extent these qualities are considered for flexible treatment is a moot question. The global scenario of pharmaceutical industry shows concentration power among a few. For instance, 53 percent market share is concentrated among the top 10 global pharma-firms handling 118 drugs, 62 percent market share in animal pharma, 80 percent share in global pesticide market and nearly 54 percent of the biotech sector's revenues. The danger of abuse of monopoly power has become real and provision for use of compulsory license is expected to be the leveraging mechanism in the hands of the developing countries. [2]

The key concern is the price of drugs post-December 2004. Studies made by WHO in 2003 indicate an upward push to prices across the spectrum. According to a study by Yale University, consumers in India are going to suffer a US$ 713 million loss in a single sub-group of anti-biotech segment. Under these circumstances, consumers in India will pay substantially higher price for drugs both out of patents well as patented. Autonomous bodies in India like national pharmaceutical pricing authority and drug price control should safeguard consumer welfare. The state therefore cannot abdicate its social justice responsibility in favour of market forces.

The copyright law's fair use provisions permit reverse engineering which is not permitted in the new patent law. This would adversely affect the patents of India, Brazil and South Africa which depend on cheap generic drugs produced in these countries.

India's Patent Amendment Bill, does not take advantage of flexibilities under TRIPS in order to safeguard accessibility and availability of drugs and medicines.

The WTO rules are complex and appear to permit some exception with countries unable to adopt measures necessary to protect public health and nutrition. It is also supposed to allow the granting of compulsory licence for production of vital drugs. It is also supposed to allow parallel importing of patented drugs i.e. their purchase from whoever sells them the cheapest. The compulsory licensing can only be obtained after efforts have been made to obtain regular licence from the patent holder on commercial terms. The result of the WTO rules effectively means government will no longer be permitted to allow local companies to process, market and export copies of patented drugs.

The impact of TRIPS will be severe on poor countries whose people cannot afford to purchase high cost patented drugs for treatment of AIDS, new strains of diseases like malaria and tuberculosis which can only be treated by recently patented drugs. WHO's study has shown that in case of pneumonia which kills 3.5 million people annually, medications that were formerly effective now fail in 70 percent of cases because of drug resistance. A new range of antibiotics is patented that will be unaffordable in developing countries.

US is using its special 301 provisions of 1988 to impose trade sanctions on countries to enforce compliance with WTO rates. High cost patented medicine does not allow poor countries like Mali, Vietnam, Colombia to spend sufficiently on building health infrastructure.

In developed countries there is widespread health insurance—Britain's spend on health per person stood at US$ 1,193 annually of which only 3 percent is paid personally. In contrast, spending per person in India is 23 percent per annum with 84 percent being paid by private households of which the cost of drugs is the highest. Increase in drug price under TRIPS will hard hit the poor. Already two billion people of the world lack access to basic health and 11 million die each year from preventable diseases. Amazingly in the eyes of US and Japan, cancer, heart complaints and asthma are not a public health problem in third world countries. Medicines only are considered; vaccines, diagnostic tests and monotony tests could not be provided cheaply under WTO rules. Clearly, the companies could not survive if their profits were to be made only on drugs for diseases mainly affecting the poorest countries.

Our new Act makes the granting of compulsory licenses for export purposes contingent upon the existence of a compulsory licence for importation in the purchasing countries.

The TRIPS Council's decision of August 30, 2004 to aid countries without manufacturing capacity to access medicines is not fully honoured by this clause since LDCs do not have to provide patents on pharmaceutical products until 2016; many of them do not have patent law institutions capable of using compulsory licences. This would make impossible for the LDCs to import drugs from India.

The root cause of rising prices, at least the branded generics was the incentive companies offer to get their drugs prescribed. Therefore, what is needed is an institutional mechanism to ensure that doctors do not prescribe expensive drugs when a cheaper alternative is available. The Government of India is willing to bring medicines in specific therapeutic segments under price control in the drug policy deliberation.

The Effects

Due to the new policy under TRIPS arrangement, the effects on our pharmaceutical industry will be as follows.

1. Our drug industries with the help of National Chemical Laboratory at Pune were producing drugs at lower cost by applying new process. The drugs were cheap. Now, thanks to the Patent Act, indigenous companies would be deprived of producing same product by applying new process.

2. In our 1972 Patent Act, the patent right was valid for 5 years. With the new Act, both prices and product patents will remain operative for 20 years. According to Hathi Committee, a newly discovered medicine is usually used for 15-20 years. The new patent right period will exceed the marketability period of drugs. A new powerful drug would appear before the expiry of the patent period. Because of this, Indian drug companies cannot reap the benefit by producing same product by applying new process. These companies have no resource to invent anything original; they could afford to produce an imitation. The new Patent Act would not give scope to do it.

3. The worst consequence of the law will be exorbitant rise in price. When Amlodipin of Pfizer company for heart disease was being sold it ₹ 26 a tablet, Indian Lyka

Company was selling same at ₹ 7. Pfizer is demanding patent of this drug. When this becomes a reality, cheaper substitute drug shall not be available.

4. The new patent law will adversely affect our pharmaceutical industry. Foreign companies will not be forced to set up their industries in our country; they would have the industries in their countries and sell the products unfettered in our country. Boots and Ciba Giegy have sold three factories in Mumbai.

Free trade encouraged by TRIPS would harm developing countries as they cannot face stiff competition of the developed countries.

Patent law in respect of pharmaceutical product is very much consequential because: (i) It will cover 22 percent of medicine according to the Indian Pharmaceutical Companies Associations, most of which are produced in India. The new Act would cover 85 to 90 percent of drugs in US and 70 to 80 percent of drugs in the world. According to Prasad and Bhat, prices of about 74 percent of drugs in India are controlled. WTO rules would loosen this control and induce price rise. UN's study shows no correlation between flow of capital and the patent law. Hence, it may not appreciably raise FDI in drug industries. (ii) Our drug industry is quite efficient. Between 1971 and 1993, sale of drugs of the foreign companies increased at a rate of 16 percent annually and sale of Indian companies rose at a rate of 26 percent per annum. Patent law may obstruct the growth of efficiency of our drug industry. [3]

Being a member of the WTO, India is under compulsion to amend its Patent Act in tune with the clauses in TRIPS Agreement. Nonetheless, keeping in view the supreme interest of our poor population and small industries, the government should incorporate some protective measures taking shelter under exception clauses and provide other incentives and permissible price regulation outside the patent.

The government should bear in mind Indira Gandhi's observation in the 1980 Conference of the WHO that invention in the field of medicine should be free of patent law and there should not be profit craze to play with the life and death of human beings. The observation of Kofi Annan, Secretary General, UN, is to be borne in mind, "striving for fair globalization means working for a process and outcomes that are fundamentally inclusive, sustainable and people-centred. Is globalization thrust in the vital field of medicine people-centred? This is the point to ponder over".

With the adoption of the product patent regime from 2005, it will now see the emergence of a single-source product. It would therefore be imperative to pre-empt the abuse of monopoly situation that invariably goes with the product patent regime. It would arrange cost benefit analysis of the new medicine to determine optimum price and the method of reference pricing. [4] Further, government should create delivery mechanism to reach the medicine to weaker sections in the remote areas of the country.

Most pharma companies boast of 20-30 percent increase in their profits year after year. Ten of 40 richest Indians are promoter of drug companies. According to a survey, over 25 percent of the rural households have to sell their land to pay for medical expenses in case of serious illness. The drug industry spends ₹ 1,10,000 per doctor per year in soliciting business. Hence, to check the profiteering of the drug companies, price control of essential drugs is a must. The foreign drug be priced in Rupee not at the rate of exchange of ₹ 40 per dollar but at purchasing power parity rate which is ₹ 8.50 a dollar. [5]

End Notes

1. Arvind Paragariya, Surrender to Multinationals, The Economic Times, 23 February, 2005.
2. J. George, The Drug Section, The Statesman, 18 December, 2004.
3. Deepak Basu, Patent Laws, The Statesman, 31 December, 2004.
4. The Economic Times, 25 August 2005, Editorial.
5. B. Sahoo, New Economic policy of India-Problems and Prospects (in Oriya), Orissa Book Store, 1997, pp. 106-109.

15

Mineral Resources and Steel Industry

Introduction

Industrialization is indispensable for rapid economic development. The pre-requisites of industrial development are availability of sufficient raw materials which are created by nature or man-made, existence of strong infrastructure and technical know-how. Nature has gifted the state of Orissa with soil and water, vast forests and plentiful of mineral resources. Some resources are renewable and some are non-renewable. Non-renewable resources consist of various minerals like iron, oil, coal, bauxite, chromite, etc. Proper use of these resources demands serious thinking on the part of the society and the state. It is the moral responsibility of the state to take into consideration, the interest of the future generations along with that of the present generation, meeting present needs and ensuring the satisfaction of the long-term needs of development. That will be called sustainable development.

Modern economic development has resulted in depletion and exhaustion of natural resources. With the spread of consumerism and rat race for economic development, the nature all over the world has been so much adversely affected that it has threatened the very existence of humanity in distant future. The realization of this grim possibility has led the thinking community to search for sustainable development path. This concern has been embodied in Rio Declaration which runs, "human beings are at the centre of concerns for sustainable development (and) are entitled to a healthy and productive life in harmony with nature".

Excessive use of minerals, materials, deforestation and excavation has led to loss of ecological balance which spells disaster on mankind. That apart, the rapidly increasing use of steel and energy poses the danger of total exhaustion of coal and iron ores in not very distant future bringing in the crisis of non-development.

Despite the spectacular knowledge revolution, such a possibility may leave us in a blind alley. That is why, it is an act of wisdom to slow down the use of non-renewable resources and avoid the crisis till an alternative to steel use and its production material is discovered to sustain economic development. The vehement public opposition to the establishment of a steel plant by South Korean steel giant at Paradeep has made this issue a burning one.

Our craze for steel industry is well known. Steel no-doubt is extremely essential for construction work, automobile production and other domestic uses. Hence, establishment of steel plants on a very large scale raises the following issues:

1. At what rate should we use the precious non-renewable minerals like iron ore and coal which are essential ingredients of steel production. While using up these resources for the benefit of the present generation, should we not consider the consequent plight of the future generations?

2. Even to the present generation what will be the cost (both private and social) of establishment of a mega plant in a place—in the form of displacement, hardship, conversion of cultivable land, destruction of green plants and pollution of air, water, etc.

3. When our indigenous industrialists and public sector steel authority are coming forward to set up such industries, why should we invite a foreign company for the purpose?

4. Even though flow of foreign direct investment is helpful to us in many a field for larger investment to step up the rate of income growth, should we allow the MNCs to enter the basic and strategic areas of production? Would it not affect our security and sovereignty?

5. Are the conditions attached to the agreement for installation of foreign company rational and conform to

level playing field?

The public has the right to get and the state has the moral duty to give satisfactory answers to these questions.

Steel Production in India

It is true that India is far behind many developed and some developing countries in respect of steel consumption and production. At the beginning of the 20th century, only 28 million tons of steel was produced all over the world. Now, the world production has reached 780 million tons. Western Europe, US, Russia, Eastern Europe and Japan are leading producers. China, South Korea, Brazil and India have expanded their production. In 2004, China produced 272 million tons of steel, Japan 112.7 million tons, US 98.4 million tons, Russia 64.3 million tons, South Korea 46.48 million tons and India 32.6 million tons of steel.

Before 1990, India's production was only 14 million tons. In developed countries, per capita per annum consumption of steel is 300 kgs., while in India, it is only 30 kgs. Consumption of steel undoubtedly is an index of level of economic and industrial development. In India's growth process, at present, contribution of industrial sector is not what it ought to be. Its contribution is only 26 percent to the total GDP while that of the services sector and agricultural sector are 54 and 18 percent respectively. Expansion of the manufacturing sector is a must and this needs more and more steel. How to meet the need is a moot point.

It is said by the steel experts that India has the potential of becoming the second largest steel producer within 15-20 years. To materialize the dream, we need enormous iron ores of good quality, coal and other minerals, in addition to adequate finance and advanced technology. Finance and technology required do not pose a problem at present.

Information is gathered that SAIL is proposing to invest ₹ 25,000 crore to raise its annual production to 11.83 million tons. Tata is proposing to expand its production by 2.4 million tons at a cost of ₹ 7,800 crore. Tata is ready to set up a 6 million tons capacity plant at Kalinga Nagar with ₹ 15,000 crore investment. Rastriya Ispat Nigam Ltd. Plans to invest ₹ 8,529 crore to double its production at Visakhapatnam from 3.5 million tons to 7 million tons, Essar Steel would expand its production at Hazira from 2.4 million tons to 4.6 million tons, Jindal would produce 3 million tons at Kharagpur, South Korea's POSCO plans to produce in Orissa 12 million tons spending US$ 12 billion. Orissa and Jharkhand with their huge deposits of iron ore are most suitable places for steel plants. Mittal is going ahead to set-up a big steel industry in Jharkhand. All these combined together amounts to huge amount of production.

In the light of the modern industrial trend, importance of steel cannot be belittled. But the question is how much iron ore deposit is there under the Earth which can sustain so much production for a long period? The following section gives an illustration to answer this question.

So far as Orissa is concerned, reserves of magnetite for iron and steel-making are not of significance.

Against the above deposits, production and export taken together were at 120.6 million tons in the country in 2003-04 and 41.86 million tons in Orissa in 2004-05.

Availability of iron ore for the iron and steel making may be assessed on the basis of the list prepared by the Steel and Mines Department indicating the details of MoUs signed and proposed to be signed. Considering the magnitude of investment and long gestation period for mega steel projects, availability of iron ore for 50 years has to be assured. Requirement of iron ore for RSPNINI, MESCO, TISCO and exports @ 10 million ton per annum for the next 5 years and @ 5 million ton per annum thereafter for 10 years and about 16 tons of iron ore feed required for production of 1 ton Hm/1 ton of DRI should be taken into consideration.

Thus, the reserves of iron ore in the state as assessed to be available on 1.4.2005 may not last for more than 30 years. Of course there is a distinct possibility of striking additional reserve with depth-wise probing. A reserve of 50 million tons was estimated by DMG and IBM during 1995-62. But till date, only 15 million tons have been extracted. Extraction becomes more difficult with increasing depth.

Orissa possesses 97.36 percent of total chromite deposits of the country and 95 percent of nickel, 77.7 percent of graphite, 50 percent of bauxite and 34 percent of iron ore.

The Mining Department of the Government of India (on the basis of extraction and state of survey knowledge) estimated in 1976-77 that the following will be the period of exhaustion; coal in 213 years, bauxite in 282 years, iron ore in 135 years, chromite in 52 years, manganese in 36 years. But in subsequent years, extraction of minerals has taken place at an alarming rate. For example, between 1994-95 and 2003-04, annual extraction of iron ore has gone up from 9.33 million tons to 34.89 million tons, coal from 32.65 million tons to 70.2 million tons and chromite from 1.25 million tons to 2.88 million tons.

With this state of mineral reserve and exploitation, how long can we sustain production and export of ores and keep mineral-based industries running?

The recent move of the Orissa Government, signing 37 MoUs for new plants of 56 million tons of annual capacity of which POSCO's share is 12 million tons has raised a big hue and cry. Doubts have been expressed regarding the materialization of the projects because of the following constraints.

1. Non-availability of high grade (65 percent Fe) lumpy ore.
2. Non-availability of good quality non-coking coal. The already serious shortage situation has been aggravated with MCL deciding to sell coal by auction.
3. Information about DRI Units in operation and/or under construction/expansion in pipeline status of NIC is sketchy and incomplete.
4. The mushrooming of DRI (SI) plants has caused severe

environmental pollution, due to the plants fault that are not installing effective pollution control devices.

Even if we assume 50 percent of the total capacity to be operational, reserve of high grade iron ore required for sponge iron making will not last for more than 20 years at best.

Kalinga Nagar tragedy in Orissa has made the situation critical and has cast a shadow over the deals. Including MESCO, the total build up in KIC is likely to be 14.5 million tons (MT). Materialization of all the new plants in KIC is unlikely due to the following reasons:

1.   Lack of access to iron ore sources.
2.   Severe environmental fallout.
3.   Acute scarcity of water.
4.   Poor infrastructure.
5.   Delay in handing over lands, free of encroachments.
6.   Poor law and order situation.

The 37 MoUs hold out the prospect of huge investment of ₹ 1,18,000 crore of which POSCO's share is ₹ 51,000 crore and that of Tata, SAIL, and Essar is ₹ 75,000 crore.

Opposition to the South Korean POSCO is also on other ground. When Tata and SAIL are planning to raise their production to 15 MT and 20MT respectively and when financial resources and technical know-how are there with our indigenous industrialists, why should we invite foreign MNCs, offering special favours?

The World Steel Dynamics of USA had placed Tata's steel production at the highest rank. POSCO no doubt has the most modern technology for producing steel at lowest cost. But statistics regarding cost or production of steel by POSCO and our native companies do not show such difference as to lure us to invite foreign companies. For example, POSCO's cost of one ton cold rolled coil is US$ 338; India's average cost is US$ 348; Tata will cost US$ 100 less. Production of hot metal is most cost effective in India. It costs US$ 100 per ton compared to US$ 117 in Brazil, US$ 132 in Russia, US$ 156 in South Korea and US$ 169 in China.

Employment Generation

The employment prospect of such mega units with severe ecological and human effect is not that bright.

Steel is no more a labour intensive industry;, POSCO employs 10,000 people for 28 MT production. Its average employment is 1,000 per MT production. SAIL employs 10,000 for one MT. Tata employs 10,000 people for 1 MT. POSCO will employ only 14,000 for 30 MT plant. But being a basic industry, both up stream and down stream employment takes place. For one unit of direct employment, indirect employment is 3.5 given the fact that half of steel production is consumed in construction and the rest is in manufacturing.

B. Mathuram of Tata opines that technology is not an edge; steel scene in the world is changing and Indian steel plants could face the change. According to A.S. Feroz, another steel expert, an additional player does not affect the market as long as demand for steel is rising. Thus, the Indian producers are not afraid of the entry of the foreign companies. What agitates the minds of the public and particularly the affected inhabitants of the proposed plant area are the rapid exhaustion of the iron ores, large scale displacement or people, adverse environmental effects and special economic zone benefit to foreign companies.

J. Mehta, Director, Essar says, "In a few years, India will badly need ore reserves for local consumption. Exhausting resources and allowing FDI for export of semi-steel may not be good in long-run".

Concluding Remarks

Our country and the state of Orissa as well are in a state of dilemma. For rapid economic development, industrial expansion is badly needed. Industrial growth in our country has not been satisfactory. Higher rate of economic growth requires infrastructural development and expansion of the manufacturing sector. For both purposes, increase in steel production is a must. But the mineral resources, iron ore and coal in the country and in the state of Orissa are not enormous enough to ensure sustainable development of the steel industry. Further, building-up of mega plants which are most cost effective but less labour-absorbing entails displacement of large number of families, majority of which are tribals and poor. In a democracy, to win the approval of the people likely to be displaced is a moral duty of the government.

The history of rehabilitation of the displaced has created distrust of the affected people. Further, along with the benefit of industrialization to the present generation, the likely dis-benefit to the future generation due to quick exhaustion of the non-renewable resources has to be considered. This calls for rational use of the natural resources. Forest degradation, water pollution and other environmental distortion have started imperilling the lives of the people. Hence, installation of industrial plants is to be done where least displacement and minimum environmental impact will occur. As Ramaswamy R. Iyer pointed out, a big project raises two issues: (i) justice and equity, and (ii) sustainability.

Keeping the above factors in view, to take a decision regarding installation of a mega plant is a challenging task. The decision-taking should not be swayed by the consideration of the interest of the powerful section of the society nor of short-term goal. Interest of the entire community and future generation should be given due weight.

While implementing the project, the concerned parties, the government and the companies should be sympathetic to the place and people and be transparent and honest in their dealing. Doing anything in haste without public debate and cautious approach would be counter productive.

16

Industrialization with Anti-Pollution Measures

Introduction

In the process of growth of an economy, industrialization holds a key position. But unfortunately, the modern pattern of industrial development with emphasis on large scale production and intensive energy use has made the Earth a 'sink' dumping ground of all wastes and residues of production and consumption and has created a situation where 'the rate of waste generation is greater than' the rate of natural assimilation. The growing menace of the mother productive activities and consumption has been well realized by the people all over the world and this realization has been echoed by the important resolution like Vienna convention, Montreal protocol, Kyoto protocol agenda 21 etc.

The mad drive for rapid industrialization has resulted in forest degradation and deterioration in the quantity of common resources like air, water and land which not only severely dims the prospect of sustainable development but also casts doubts on the survival of the humanity.

The Neoclassical economists like Jevon, Edgeworth-Marshall, Pareto, Pigou with their marginal analysis drew our attention to the 'environmental economics' and the modern economists developing the study of environment emphasized that human population, unplanned urbanization, deforestation profit oriented capitalism and technological advancement are responsible for the pollution crisis on Earth. Accelerated economic development has been associated with the exhaustion of natural resources and deterioration of the ecology. Economists have started studying the cost and benefit of the modern development and have attempted to devise ways of at least reducing the menacing effect of such productive process.

A few decades back, developing countries like India where poverty and penury are widespread and natural resources were unutilized, ecological problem was pushed to the background and development in all sectors with application of modern technology was a dire necessity. Now with the elimination of distressing poverty and generation of hope for improving the standard of living matching that of the developed world, the issue of ecological balance has raised its head.

Economists and the scientists have started assessing the environmental effects of the modern productive activities. The assessment has run mostly in terms of physical realities—the psychological aftermaths of environmental degradation have not been fully grasped. Attempts are being made to impose standards for emission of different pollutants for different industries and polluters pay principle or 'PPP' has been applied to make pollutants bear the cost of the measures taken to reduce pollution to levels specified by public authorities. [1] Market-based instruments, taxes and incentives are being used to regulate and reduce pollution. Under marketable pollution permits, the regulating authority issues tradable permits for a certain level of pollutants emitted by the polluters. [2]

Changes in production technology have been sought in favour of installing clean technology. In spite of all these attempts, the environmental problems go on haunting both developed and developing countries.

Pollution has engulfed cities as well as country side. The problem is becoming unmanageable in some cities of our country. The most pollution affected cities in India are Bhopal, Bangalore, Chennai, Delhi, Hyderabad, Mumbai, Ahmedabad, Jaipur, Guwahati, Kolkata, Assonsol, Durgapur and Bhubaneswar. The cities have been polluted mostly due to industrial and vehicular emissions. Incidence of water borne diseases due to water pollution and pollution of the land due to mining activities has gone beyond the periphery of the cities.

The awareness of environmental degradation has created great concern for sustainable development amongst the technologists and statesmen. Achieving sustainability in industrialized nations means transportation without smog, consumer goods without toxic wastes, energy without acid rain etc. [3] The conventional energy now being used like coal, petrol etc. are both scarce and non-renewable resources. How to conserve natural resources for future consumption, avoid misuse, over exploitation and harness alternative and non-conventional sources of energy through technological innovation are goals earnestly pursued by the industrialized and industrializing countries.

The onus of responsibility to save the humanity and civilization squarely lies on the highly industrialized and rapidly industrializing countries because these countries at present account for the major shares on ecological imbalances created on Earth.

The Earth is under two attacks namely: (a) excessive demand and wasteful habits of affluent population, and (b) billions of new mouths in developing countries.

Industrial countries with 21 percent of world population consume 85 percent of world's metal and chemicals, 92 percent of cars, 81 percent of paper, 82 percent of gasoline, 72 percent of diesel and 85 percent of gas. They are responsible for 70 percent of emission. [4]

Increasing damage is done to the ecology of our country because of non-adoption of measures to check or abate pollution effects of industrial and mineral excavation activities. The greatest environmental tragedy in India had appeared in Bhopal in the form of gas leakage from a Union Carbide factory in 1984 which killed 10,000 victims in one week and rendered others morbid. This is surely a sign of sheer neglect of industrialists to take adequate precautionary measures. Kirit Parikh et al. in a study integrating natural resources accounting with traditional economic accounting have drawn our attention to the association of emission and effluents with various economic activities. [5] A report published by National Environmental Engineering Research Institute (NEERI), Research and Development Division showed that when accounting for environmental degradation was integrated with economic accounts of India, then the adjusted annual growth rate in gross domestic product appeared to be negative instead of being positive during the period 1980-90 to 1991-95. [6]

Government's pro-business policy since 1980s has raised the share of corporate investment in GDP and private sector companies have grown at a relatively rapid pace during 1980s. The paid-up capital of private companies grew at an average rate of 7.3 percent in 1970s, whereas the growth rate during 1980s was 14.3 percent. Also, the number of private companies during 1980s grew at an annual rate of 13.5 percent compared to a growth rate of 3.3 percent for the public sector companies. [7]

Between 1980-81 and 2004-05, GDP multiplied by 3.81 and GDP per capita multiplied by 2.37. During this period, GDP at factor cost in 1993-94 prices increased from ₹ 4,011 billion to ₹ 15,294 billion while GDP per capita increased from ₹ 5,908 to ₹ 14,018. [8] The rate of growth of the Indian economy has been much higher than that of the western economies. Rapid growth of income has created a craze for industrial products like automobiles which is sure to add to environmental degradation unless preventive measures are taken. Rising corporate sector which has an innate desire for greater profit is likely to pay less attention to environmental protection.

Environmental degradation in Orissa due to industrialization and other causes has not been duly measured. Nirmal Chandra Sahu has assessed the damage inflicted by environmental problem in the Angul Talcher region in Orissa. [9] The state of Orissa encounters perplexing dilemma of development versus healthy environment growth. Though industrially as well as agriculturally a mach backward state, the nature and spatial character of some of its development projects poses a conflict between development and environmental protection.

Water pollution from industries, mines, agricultural fields is causing great concern in Orissa. Brahmani water has become poisonous and water quality deterioration is high near industrial complexes like Rourkela, Angul and Talcher. Large quantities of pesticide and agrochemicals find their way into Chilika through many rivers, rivulets and surface run off.

Environmental degradation in mining area is caused by methods of mining ore beneficiation, soil sub-soil/slope destabilization, pollution of water resources, solid waste tailing etc. All these are found in surface mining of Talcher, Bonai-Keonjhar. Effluents from industries of a mining area add pollution and waste to neighbouring areas.

Pollution is being caused by a number of industries in the state having no sufficient preventive measures. The volume of effluents discharged from Aska Sugar Mills is enormous— process time's effluent and cooling powder and excess condensate emanate from a sugar mill. The state environment pollution control board reports that no distillery in Orissa has adequate spent-worth treatment facility. Effluent treatment facilities in some paper mills are very inadequate. Hira Cement, Bargarh continues to operate in the wet process without any electro-static precipitator in its kiln. The factory is a major air pollutant in the area.

Rourkela Steel Plant is a major pollutant in Rourkela. The incessant emission of various types of gases from the steel plant and other industries has resulted in large-scale pollution of land, air, and water. 14.8 persons per thousand suffer from water borne diseases and 4.8 persons from asthma in Rourkela town. The three units of the smelter units of NALCO emit gases which may be harmful. The State Pollution Control Board is continuously monitoring the boilers performa, the stroke emission and the ambient equation of various places within Talcher town. Measures taken by Talcher Power Station have averted pollution effect so far. [10]

The state is not yet an industrially developed state. The share of the manufacturing sector in the NSDP which was 7.22 percent in 1993-94 declined to 5.31 percent in 1997-98 and to 4.94 percent in 2003-04. [11] But the state government is trying hard to accelerate industrial development with the help of its enormous mineral resources. So far, 46 MoUs have been signed for setting up steel, aluminium and oil industries. These mega projects when implemented, will pose formidable environmental problems.

Studies made by West Bengal Pollution Control Board shows that air pollution has taken place in Asansol where IISCO steel plant exists and in Durgapur with SAIL's steel plant is located. The ambient air quality standard for SPM (suspended particulate matter) is fixed at 2000g/m for residential areas. But the rate of exception of this permissible varies from 2 to 38 percent at times in Asansol and SPM for Durgapur exceeded by 70.8 percent. Due to inadequacy of water, 1,70,000 persons in Durgapur and 1,38,871 persons in Asansol are placed at a disadvantage. Huge flyash and other ash products are generated at Durgapur. The effects of air and water pollution are enormous. In Asansol, in 1972, 37.02 percent of the patients suffered from respiratory diseases and 43.3 percent patients suffered from gastrointestinal diseases. In the same year, 60 percent of this suffering was attributed to air and water pollution. The mortality rate at Durgapur was 14.6 per thousand. [12]

The current capacity of iron and steel plants in Orissa stands at 4.7 million tones and when the MoUs are signed and implemented, the capacity of iron and steel production in Kalinga Nagar industrial complex will be 14.5 million tonnes. [13] The huge production is sure to pose an environmental challenge.

Burning of fossil fuels release six billion tonnes of carbon dioxide in the world. This adds to global warming. Fossil fuels in thermal power plant produce sulphur dioxide and oxides of nitrogen which causes acid rain.

It is now crystal clear that environmental protection is an integral part of all developmental programmes and it is an issue vital to all countries, rich or poor. It is also increasingly realized that continuing neglect of ecology could spell disaster to the humanity. Mark Arnett of Environment, Nuclear Safety and Civil protection, Brussels rightly says, "The aim now is to match our future production and consumption pattern so that the environment can sustain in the long term".

Economic development requires more and more exploitation of minerals, but exploitation, without proper safety measures causes heavy social cost in the form of environmental damage. The economic policies of the states seem to attach no importance to the critical environmental appraisal process which industries must go thorough. [14]

Assessment of damage done to the resources and recovery of the cost is essential. The US Department of Interior said that damages should be equal to: (i) lost value of the resources, or (ii) the value of restoring the resources to its former state. Scholars have attempted to measure the abatement cost of waste water, air pollution, disposal of solid waste in Asansol and Durgapur. [15] Similar assessment should be made in cities where mega industries are set up and recovery of the cost has to be made from concerned industries. Preventive policy and clean technology have to be adopted in existing and new industries as has been done in Durgapur Steel Plant.

Environmental damage abatement measures and anti-pollution measures would improve quality of life by restoring some of the lost quality of air and water. Recycling of residuals and waste material, waste energy should be made an integral part of industrial activities. The study regarding Durgapur Steel Plant reveals that decentralized environmental policy-suasion market pricing etc., produced better results than centralized policy-governmental regulation and intervention.

Keeping in view the declaration in 'India Development Report 1999-2000" we are to take appropriate steps to mitigate industrial pollution. The report said, 'Air and water pollution imposes enormous burden on people's health. The costs of cleaning up air and water are comparatively small, clean air and water is not a luxury, they are a necessity to sensible policies, right to information, citizen awareness, and a lot of investment, we should and must clean up our air and water".

In our country there is Central Pollution Control Board and State Pollution Control Boards to prevent, control and abate environmental pollution in the country, According to P.M. Prasad, since the market and liability systems are unable to provide incentives to the polluter to reduce pollution, the regulatory system has to be strengthened and pollution control boards are to be empowered to impose a fine against rogue industries. [16]

End Notes

1.   H.M. Dixit, Environmental Pollution, 1990, and A. K. Dasgupta, Economist of Political Economy, 1993.

2.   See Ian Bateman, Environmental and Economic Appraisal; Environmental Science and Environmental Management, 1995. Anil Markandy, Market-based Instruments for Environmental policies in Developing Countries, Upgradation courses on Environmental Economics, 2000. Pearce and Turner, Economics of Natural Resources and the Environment, 1990.

3.   H. Edward Stead and Jesn Gamer Stead, Strategic Management for a Small Planet, Business and Environment, 1999.

4.   Kirit Parikh, RIO-What the Rich did not want to Hear?, Economic Times, July 20, 1992.

5.   Kirit S. Parikh, Yotik Parikh, V. K. Sharma and J.P. Painuly, Natural Resources Accounting- A Framework for India, The Challenge of the Balance, (ed.) by Amit Agarwal, 1997.

6.   National Environmental Engineering Research Institute (NEERT), 1997.

7.   Atul Kohli, Politics of Economic Growth in India, 1980-2005, EPW, April 1, 2006.

8.   Deepak Nayyar, Economic Growth in Independent India, EPW, April 15, 2006, pp. 1446-1448.

9.   Nirmal Chandra Sahu, Economics of Pollution-A Case Study of Angul-Talcher Industrial region in Orissa, Upgradation courses in Environmental Economics, 1999.

10. Basudeb Sahoo, Economics of Environments-A Socio-political-cultural Study, R. Meher, Industry versus Environment-The Case Study of Rourkela, Environment and Economic Development, 1996, pp. 125-130 and 164-165.

11. Economic Survey, 2005-06, Government of Orissa.

12. Ghosh, Bose and Associates, Environmental Management Plan of Asansol-Durgapur Industrial Corridor, May, 1997.

13. See Memorandum of Understanding between Government of Orissa and M/s POSCO, Republic of Korea, June 22, 2005.

14. Ashok Kothari, Environment and New Economic Policies, EPW, April 29, 1995, p. 1928.

15. Pritha Goswami, Economics of Environment-A Study of Durgapur Industrial Region, Unpublished Ph.D. thesis, Visva Bharati University, 2002.

16. P.M. Prasad, Environment Protection-Role of Regulatory System in India, EPW, April 1, 2006, p. 1287.

17

Alienation, Displacement and Rehabilitation

Despite various land reform acts ensuring security of tenants, preventing land alienation, particularly in respect of scheduled caste and scheduled tribe land owners and providing equivalent land and appropriate rehabilitation of the displaced persons, the problems of alienation, dispossession and non-rehabilitation continue to exist creating acute discontent amongst the affected persons. The socio-economic conditions of the schedule caste and schedule tribe people are so miserable and they are so disorganized that fraudulent practices and unethical activities concerning lands possessed by them go on unchecked. Non-implementation of laws passed by the Government, thanks to the nefarious activities of the vested interest and unsympathetic attitude of the administrative and legal officers, is the greatest stumbling block on the path of cherished goal of reforms.

Land Alienation

Land alienation means alienating the possessor of land from the land holding. This dispossession may take place legally or illegally. Legal alienation occurs when pressed by circumstances, the owner of the land on his own accord sells away his land to meet some contingencies. Such selling away one's entitlement is easy when there is no legal bar. But in some cases, particularly in case of schedule castes and tribes, there are certain rules restricting and prohibiting sale of land to the non-scheduled persons. The issue becomes serious when a prospective buyer belonging to general caste taking advantage of the poverty of the scheduled land owner, tempts him or forces him to sell away the land and the sub-registrar legalizing the sale deed is bribed to close his eyes against the violation of the law.

A number of acts have been passed in our country and the states to protect the land ownership of the vulnerable sections of the society.

As far back as in 1917, Agency Tracts Interest and Land Transfer Act of 1917 came into force on August 14, 1947. The Act covered the agency areas of Koraput, Ganjam and Phulbani. Article 19 of the Indian Constitution prohibits transfer of land of the scheduled castes and scheduled tribes to the general population. Administration of Orissa State Order 1948, the Orissa Scheduled Areas Transfer of Immovable Property Regulation 1958, and OLR Act, 1960 and 1965 (amended) provide numerous checks to easy transfer of lands of the scheduled population to the general ones.

44.5 percent of Orissa's land area constitutes scheduled area. Tribal cultivators number 9.25 lakh. In addition, there are 2 lakh families practicing poduchasa. Tribal agricultural labourers numbered 6.5 lakh in 1991.

There are no special land rights for the tribals. The tribals could not avail of the general pattern of land rights conferment due to ignorance and poverty. Attempts have been made to check land alienation of tribals since Durbar administration. Keonjhar prohibited colonization of Bhuyanpir and Jhangpir area. Land alienation was prohibited in Koraput and Ganjam agency areas under Agency Tracts and Land Transfer Act of 1917. C.P. Tenancy Act also protected tribal land holders in Sambalpur. Since Independence, various acts as mentioned earlier have checked land alienation.

By 1991, 87,500 cases of illegal transfer of tribal lands were registered. Koraput, Phulbani, Ganjam and Mayurbhanj districts accounted for 50 percent of cases ending in 43.5 percent of eviction. Areas ordered for restoration to the original tribal owner amounted to 3,153 acres. Actual restoration was 27,633 acres i.e. 88.7 percent of area ordered for restoration area out of the purview of 1.7 lakh acres.

The tribals have no written right on forestland. The intermediaries purchased whatever land the tribals possessed at the time of *Zamindari* abolition. The 1965 Act prevented illegal transfer and as per the law, the affected party can seek remedy within 12 years of illegal possession since 1975.

The laws passed have not benefited the tribals as expected because of the following reasons.

1. First, there is no record of right in the possession of the tribals.
2. Second, lot of *benami* transfers have taken place; land has been transferred from real owner to another tribal but in fact the land is cultivated or used by the non-tribals.
3. Third, the powerful families in the scheduled areas have won over the judges and their collusion has resulted in dispossession of tribals.
4. Fourth, the tribals are not well organized to protect their rights and revolt against the vested interests.
5. Fifth, the wretched economic condition and ignorance of law facilitates the illegal transfer of land.

To stop land alienation and protect the interests of the tribals the acts should be amended for quick disposal of cases.

The onus of proof or disproof should lie on the buyer not the poor seller. The law would give enough power to the SDO, and the local officer to finalise the dispute. Shyness and reluctance of the tribals should be removed and a sense of right be created amongst them through proper education and awareness campaign by political parties and voluntary organizations.

Displacement and Rehabilitation

Displacement of tribals has been indispensable for execution of any development project undertaken in tribal areas. Most of our development projects, river, dam, mineral based industries or construction of road into the interior of forest and hilly areas has involved massive displacement.

Development has been perceived as a battery of changes

for the betterment of the community. It involves the notion of progress, growth, upliftment and collective welfare. Both in the process of the development, of the collectivity, a number of families, mostly poor, inarticulate have been victimized. Development is no longer understood in terms of statistical indices, political symbols, economic parameters; it is more and more understood in terms of quality of life, locally felt culturally conditioned individual and group needs.

Installation of heavy industries and construction of big dams mostly taking place in inaccessible tribal areas have served the interests of the advanced communities and caused break-down of the social network and creation of the cultural diaspora of the tribal.

Studies of displacement and resettlement conducted in many third world and developing nations such as Brazil, Indonesia and Kenya report disappointing experience. In Brazil, dam on lakes Obracinto displaced 65,000 people that had disastrous socio-economic consequences. In Indonesia, local people refused to move out of the reservoir areas of Kedangaumbo dam. In Kenya's Klambere reservoir, the settlers' average land holding diminished to less than half and their livestock was reduced by more than a third and more than 33 percent of settlers were without new houses by the end of the project. In Nepal, a majority of the families displaced from Kulkarni reservoir became poorer after dislocation.

Displacement of people from their traditional habitat in Orissa has been studied by Roy Burman Kave and Kinbker. According to N.K. Behera, L.K. Mohapatra and S.M. Patnaik, "Since 1980s the issues have been linked up with issue of human rights and has acquired new dimensions". [1]

The upper Kolab project in Koraput district affected 147 villages covering total are of 9,076 h.a. and needing rehabilitation of 5,366 families. They were to be rehabilitated in Kotapad Tehsil 70 km. away from the dam site.

The Government of Orissa formulated uniform rehabilitation policy for major and medium projects in 1972.

The policy contained, namely.

1. Each displaced family would be allotted three acres of reclaimed irrigated land or 6 acres of reclaimed unirrigated land; fifty percent reclamation cost be recovered from the allotter subject to a maximum of ₹ 300 per acre.
2. Each displaced family would be allotted 0.50 acres of land for house site.
3. Free transport of household belongings would be provided.
4. In the resettlement colonies essential public amenities like roads, wells, ponds and schools be provided.
5. In 1983, government decided that wherever land is not available, rehabilitation grants be paid at the rate of ₹ 2,160 per acre of unirrigated land.
6. No submersion be allowed till the rehabilitation facilities are provided.
7. Displaced families recovering compensation of ₹ 50,000 or above would be required to pay full cost of reclamation at the time of payment.
8. No redemption cost would be realized from displaced families who are landless.

Rehabilitation was complete by 1987. The study of S.M. Patnaik revealed that the target oriented approach of the Government officers compelled them to adopt unscrupulous methods of divide and rule and physical force which created psychological damage, collective frustration, trauma, disgust and mistrust towards the *Sarkar Lok*. In the rehabilitation colony, the tribals faced several hardships like lack of fuel, wood, water, problem of conjugal adjustment and selection of life partner, changes in dress patterns, hair style, use of cosmetics. However, the basic ethnic group specific culture continued.

In 2006, the Government of Orissa enacted a law regarding rehabilitation in which the following items stood prominent.

1. The companies were allowed to acquire private lands directly without the intermediation of the government.

2. The displaced persons can have a stake in the company by purchasing a share.
3. One person from each displaced family is assured of a job.
4. A displaced family would get an assistance of ₹ 1.5 lakh for construction of a house.
5. Kalinga Nagar and Posco displaced persons will get some special benefits.
6. There would be a directorate to monitor the implementation of the Act.
7. There would be committees at state and district level for land acquisition and rehabilitation.

A family not getting a job would get special compensation of one to five lakh rupees. If the family invests 50 percent of the compensation, it will be entitled to be share holder of the company. There will be rehabilitation and peripheral development and advisory committee whose consultation is indispensable for displacement and rehabilitation. The displaced persons will be given some land for cultivation.

Those who would not take land, would get compensation at the rate of ₹ 1 lakh an acre of irrigated and ₹ 50,000 for an acre of unirrigated land. The betel vine cultivators in Posco area numbering 1900 would get compensation at the rate of ₹ 6,000 per one decimal land. In Kalinga Nagar, the displaced persons will get ₹ 50,000 per acre as compensation. There will be advertisement for state level displacement and rehabilitation and a state level council consisting of the chief minister, concerned minister, parliamentarian, environmentalist, and intellectuals.

The Rural Development Ministry of the Government of India has made rules for rehabilitation. Land is acquired for development project on the basis of the amended 1984 Land Acquisition Act under which government can acquire private land for use. Further, compensation is paid only for land on which there is legal right. Most tribals having no legal document of possession are deprived of compensation benefit. About 5 lakh people every year are displaced for planned development. These displaced persons are becoming poorer.

Failed Laws

Not withstanding the laws passed to rehabilitate the displaced as suitably as possible, the reality of the post displacement is quite grim. Statistics regarding displacement and rehabilitation give a harrowing picture.

It is commonly felt that the big project undertaken for accelerated economic development has caused transfer of wealth from the poor to the rich, from the have nots to the have lots.

Whatever statistics are available from the government records reveal that since 1951 to 1990, displaced persons in the country varied from 10 lakh to 185 lakh; some say the number may be about 2.13 crore. Counted indirectly, the affected numbers may go up to 4 crore.

Out of the 213 lakh displaced persons, 25.5 lakh are due to mines, 12.5 lakh due to industry, 174 lakh due to big and medium river projects and 7 lakh due to recreation gardens.

Between 1951 and 1990, 3,643 river embankment projects have been implemented and about 53.09 lakh people have been displaced by medium river projects. Most of the displaced persons are scheduled caste and scheduled tribe people and small farmers. About 13.3 lakh tribals have been displaced due to mineral excavation.

The Centre for Science for Environment (CSE) reports that out of 30 thousand people displaced in Vacra Nangal Project, only 12,000 have been rehabilitated.

In Utkal Project, 18,500 were displaced out of which 3,000 have been rehabilitated. Pongdam Project resulted in 33,000 displaced people of which only 9,000 have been rehabilitated; of the total displaced persons only 27.5 percent are rehabilitated.

Expenditure on rehabilitation of displaced persons of river projects is only 1 percent of the project cost. The cost of constructing the temporary houses employees of Sardar

Sarover River project is more than compensation for one lakh displaced person.

The Government has not been very sympathetic to the displaced persons. Proper thinking has not been given to the issue and exact estimation of the number of persons to be displaced and the loss they would incur has not been made. The rate of compensation has not been based on market value of the assets and compensation has been paid after many years. The displaced persons of Vakranangal Project (1942-47) got their compensation in 1952-57. The compensation payment has been substantially pocketed by unscrupulous officers and touts.

There has been gender discrimination in matters of compensation payment, while paying compensation the government has not properly advised the tribals how to spend the money. Compensation money has been unproductively spent by the tribals. A survey shows that the displaced persons of Sriram Nagar spent only 4 percent of compensation on land-purchase, 20 percent on dress, 25 percent on loan payment and 50 percent on household consumption.

Displacement has added to the miseries of the poor tribals. Besides this, it has caused havoc to the environment, created massive unemployment and loss of common property. The mental agony of the displaced is immeasurable—uprooted from their natural habitat they have lost their lifestyle and culture.

In Talcher area, acquisition of five villages has resulted in 43.6 percent unemployment amongst the displaced villagers. The number of landless among displaced persons of Rengali River project has doubled. Singarali coalmines have raised displaced persons by 20 to 72 persons. Because of displacement in two other projects the ownership of common land has declined from 23.2 percent to 16.5 percent.

Considering the hardship and inequality caused by displacement, a suitable displacement policy has to be formulated and the matter be placed under concurrent list of the Constitution, said Sri Braja Tripathy the former minister.

With the killings of tribals in Kalinga Nagar, Odisha's concern for the would be displaced has increased. The archaic land laws and lack of political will and inapt administration has added to the problem.

The problems of urban and rural displacement are different. Displacement in urban areas is predominantly due to encroachment. It is estimated that 55 percent of Mumbai's population lives in 2500 slums; of this, 50 percent of slums on private land, 25 percent on state government land, 20 percent on municipal land, 5.5 percent on central government land and airport land. Mumbai has witnessed 80,000 families whose rehabilitation will cost ₹ 2,500 crore.

In Kalinga Nagar, 700 families have been evicted from their villages without resettlement plan. 50 percent of families having no record of rights and are denied compensation. Police force is used to constitute Gram Sabha where consent is manufactured. The companies acquire much more land they require. Pohang Steel Company is set to acquire 4800 hectares of prime land for its plant in Orissa. Thousand acres of land are under the possession of the politicians which are underused. These lands should first be acquired for setting up plants there.

The Draft National Policy on Resettlement and Rehabilitation rightly states: (i) that negotiation should primarily be conducted between the party building the private project and the people being displaced with the government acting as a facilitator. The displaced are to be given some stake in the project where possible, (ii) a portion of the revenue earned from the project should be spent for development of the locality, (iii) rehabilitation bodies should take care that displaced villages are settled as a unit and not fragmented, (iv) a corresponding commission would analyse the issues, (v) the Archaic Land Acquisition Act needs a revamp and state government should maintain better land records, and (vi) compensation be paid for acquired land at the market price. [2]

If the industrialization and modernization are to be taken up, one has to enter first into a dialogue with the people who will be affected by such development and work out a plan with them on how this is to be done. [3]

To compete with the rest of the world under the WTO regime, huge infrastructure has to be built up. This involves uprooting lot of people from their habitat. To lessen the discontent of the affected people, lot of brainstorming of the planners is needed. Sentiments play huge psychological role. Large projects have been opposed. To tackle the issues, a number of institutional arrangements may be made to take care of the future needs of people whose present house sites will have to be acquired so that the dislodged will not be described as victims of development. The institutional arrangement should contain political representatives, policymakers, think-tanks and social activists. Taking a futuristic approach for determinating the prices of the sites will yield better results and avoid social unrest. [4]

End Notes

1. S.M. Patnaik, Displacement Rehabilitation and Social Change, Inter-India Publications 1996, pp. 22-28.
2. Deepak Parikh, Chairman, HDFC, Economic Times, 7th February, 2006.
3. Actiyut Das, Agragamee, Koraput, Economic Times, 7th February, 2006.
4. Anilek Agrawal, Assocham, Economic Times, 7th February, 2006.

18

Climate Change and Development Perspective

The whole world is terribly concerned over ecological imbalance and is striving for an effective remedy without discernible success. Since 2007, following the publication of the IPCC Report under the Chairmanship of Dr. R.K. Pachauri, our attention has been focused on climate change which is increasingly felt by the common men of the world. The external manifestation of change in the atmosphere and its impact on Earth has generated a sense of horror among the conscious people.

Here is an attempt: (i) to highlight the nature and speed of climate change in recent years and to probe into the causes, (ii) to delineate its present impact and point out the future consequences, and (iii) to bring out a road map to check the disastrous consequences.

Present Scenario

The climate change which we observe today may be attributed to causes over which we have no control and factors which are man-made. Warming of the Earth is the root cause of climate change and to certain extent it is due to the increase in Carbon emission in recent years. There is of course, a strong argument that man cannot alter the cyclical pattern of climatic changes that can be brought about by nature—changes in the Earth's magnetic field and the long cycle of warming and freezing. The sudden change in the Earth's magnetic field may occur at regular intervals in every 26,000-30,000 years—changing the climate dramatically and instantly would allow a few human beings to survive. The changes in Earth's magnetic field cause changes in geographic distribution—galactic and solar cosmic rays causing increase in the death rates of oceanic plant life which destroys carbon. This in turn increases the global warming process. The Earth has experienced warm periods in the past including the medieval warm period (800-1300 A.D.), the md-Holocene (600 years ago) and the penultimate interglacial period (1,25,000 years ago). The Earth 1,30,000 years ago was much warmer than today and a substantial portion was then under water. [1]

Radiation from the Sun or the Earth's natural temperature cycle and accumulation of Co2 in the atmosphere are thought to be the cause of global warming. The present climate change is linked with the use of coal and oil for power generation. At present, oil accounts for 45 percent of global carbon emission, coal for 37 percent and natural gas for 10 percent. Coal and oil are expected to remain dominant sources of energy for the next 50 years. Humankind will have to exploit renewable energy of the Sun. The present reliance on coal can be gauged from the fact that the US gets 43 percent of its energy from coal and is expected to build another 280 coal fixed power plants with a capacity of 500 MW each between 2003-2030. China is building one such plant every week or 26GW per year. All this puts a premium on carbon capture and storage.

In Denmark, the Eberg Power Station has implemented carbon capture resulting in negligible carbon emission. All these techniques increase the fuel needs of power plant by 25-40 percent and add to the cost of power by 25-90 percent. But this oceanic storage will have adverse environmental impact. Carbon sequestration by using plantation is nature's way of combating the problem and this is done in China and Ethiopia. [2] Nuclear power results in up to 25 times more carbon emission than wind energy. The disadvantages of nuclear power as pointed out in a report by MIT are high capital cost, long installation time and the cost of safe disposal and storage of nuclear waste. Since 2000, only 2000 MW of nuclear power has come on lines. Hydroelectricity is a form of renewable energy free of carbon emission. Worldwide, there was an installed capacity of 777 GW which supplied 2998 TWh in 2006. This was about 20 percent of the world capacity and accounted for 88 percent of electricity from renewable sources. India has enormous potential for generation of hydroelectric power and currently exploits only 15 percent. But then hydroelectric generation involves huge displacement and ecological impact.

Challenges before the Developing Countries

The developing countries face challenges of poverty and global climate change. Voluntary commitment and the dreams of self-regulation will not yield desirable results. Market-economy hardly can mitigate the evil effects of climate change. Locational climatic effect and the economic activities cannot be voluntarily linked. The problem calls for threadbare discussion among nations and deep commitment. The stage is open to put in place a sufficiently dynamic regulatory regime that can bring accountability in response to global climate change. The poor in the poor country are the worst victims of climate change. The goals of amelioration of poverty and reduction of carbon emission often conflict with each other. [3]

Most populous countries like China and India have a big stake in deciding how much carbon emission they could reduce. India stands one rank below US and sixth in world pecking order in green house gases emission. China has declared voluntary reduction in carbon intensity by 40-45 percent by 2020. India has announced to cut down carbon intensity by 20-25 percent. This is achievable with GDP growth of 8-9 percent, with application of right technology. But China and India are not ready to subject themselves to international verification. The targets set by India will be in accordance to its resources and social-economic priorities.

As per Soma Banerjee, the biggest Green House Gas producer in world is China sharing 20.7 percent of global emission, US is the second with 15.55 percent of total emission, EU is third with 11.9 percent of emission and India is sixth with 5 percent of global emission. But India's per head emission is just 2 tonnes of carbon dioxide (66th in world) where as US is 5th with 20 tonnes per head carbon dioxide emission. The United Nations Framework Commission on Climate Change (UNFCCC) speaks of differentiated responsibility to reduce emission to which US opposes. [4]

There are different views on sharing responsibility. The Third world asks the developed countries to arrest global warming. The developed countries forced the poor countries to observe the stringent criteria for sustainable development. Indira Gandhi 30 years back said, "Poverty is the biggest enemy of the environment". Anthony Giddens writes in his classic book, "Poorer countries must have the right to develop economically even if this process involved a significant growth in green house gases". Wiel Hutton observed in the Observer, 'Poor countries must burn coal. To ask the entire world to commit to sustainable development is to damn the less developed world to poverty".

In the poorest countries in Africa, life expectancy is as low as 37 years, adult literacy is 17 percent and GDP per capita is US$ 470. International funding agencies are refusing to finance projects in Laos, Vietnam and Uganda on sustainability ground. Stringent conditions regarding environment protection stand on the path of economic development of the poor countries. [5]

Scientists are not sure of the rate at which global warming will change, yet it is happening—prudent people will take out insurance against a catastrophe that may never happen. The cost of limiting carbon emission can be viewed as a worthwhile insurance premium. [6]

If carbon is the catastrophic culprit, the polluter has to pay. But then the question is on what basis, countries would pay the penalty, on absolute emission or per capita emission or historical accumulation?

If we view carbon as a possible pollutant, not a proven one, then it becomes more difficult to decide who should pay what premium. The insurance premium approach views all countries to be beneficiary of emission reduction and therefore have to share the responsibility. Populous countries like China and India obviously reject this approach. Besides, carbon dioxide and other gases (notably methane) also contribute to green house gases. Methane comes from rice, sheep and cattle. Rice growers have been putting methane into atmosphere, since thousand years, while industrialized countries have been putting carbon dioxide since about 250 years. All these considerations makes it difficult to have an agreement on sharing responsibility.

Progress in carbon reduction is halted due to above controversy. In Kyoto Convention in 1977, all countries signed to cut carbon emission. Virtually nothing has been done in that regard. Supposing 1990 global index was 100, without Kyoto, it would be have been 142.7 in 2010, with Kyoto convention it is 142.2 and with Kyoto implementation it would have been 133. The Kyoto promise failed because it is expensive to cut carbon emissions. That is why Bjora Lomberg suggested to focus efforts in making non polluting energy sources cheaper than fossil fuels and spend 0.2 percent of global GDP or US$ 100 billion a year on green energy research. But this approach did not figure in Copenhagen—A smarter strategy than the one dogmatically pursued in Copenhagen is needed. [7]

Varying Views on Measures for Solution

Human action may not be wholly responsible for global warming, but it has intensified the warming process. It can be reversed if we change our life style and the method of energy generation.

There are three viable solutions: (a) the fast breeder nuclear reactors can use natural uranium only in the first style. It can then produce plutonium from the waste products to make these reactors self-sufficient, (b) the other alternative is what the Russian scientists have proposed in the 1988— specifically to set up a joint solar reflector in outer space to reflect the Sun's energy to the Earth. This can produce all the energy the world needs without using the fossil fuels. That can slow down the warming process without sacrificing the life style of the industrialized societies. The technical design has been developed by the physico-technical Institute of Russian Academy of Science, (c) the third scientific solution is to put a massive amount of sulphur dioxide in the upper atmosphere of the Earth to cool down the temperature by 2-3 degrees below the current level.

Under the Kyoto Protocol, market-based solution can at best reduce carbon emission levels by 4-7 percent below the 1990 levels. However, it is not a solution to the problem of global warming. [8]

In February 2010, a group of 14 distinguished climate scientist headed by Gwyn Prince of London School of Economics published a report titled, The Hartwell. It was noted that 18 years of the Kyoto Protocol approach to international climate policy have failed to produce discernible real-world reduction in emission of green house gases. The paper said, climate change is much more complicated, involving open, complex and imperfectly understood system. It is not a conventional environmental problem. It is as much an energy problem as an economic development problem or a land use problem. The scientists point out that there are four policy levers to lower carbon emission and rein in climate change, reducing the world population, shrinking the global economy, increasing the efficiency of energy consumption and decreasing carbon intensity Reducing global population is implausible and reducing size of the global economy would result in increased hardship for billions.

The Hartwell Group proposes that we adopt three basic climate related goals, ensuring secure affordable energy supplies for everyone alternative to fossil fuels—ensuring that economic development does not wreak environmental havoc— cutting indoor pollution from burning biomass, reducing ozone and protecting tropical forests and making sure that we are prepared to cope with whatever climate changes may occur.

Hartwell Group throws out a wide approach adoption, reforestation, encouraging biodiversity and improving air quality. The paper observes 'we need to ignite an energy technology revolution. Kyoto type of all inclusive approach needs to be broken into separate issues. [9]

All these measures are needed because we fear that carbon emission unchecked will usher in doom's day. But Bjorn Lomborg thinks it is illusions of Armageddon. A sea level rise of 5 meters will affect according to Lomborg about 400 million people and force relocation of 15 million people. Realistic approach to climate change requires abandoning our fixation in farfetched Armageddon scenario. [10]

Many scientists feel that innovation and invention of new technology can solve the energy problem without harmful emission. Teri Mckinsey and number of IIT studies confirm this view. Village scale biomass and rural photovoltaic system can offer energy services to 40 percent of Indian population.

Efficient use and renewable energy technology would go a long way to meet the crisis. Solar and wind energy as being priortised in Germany and Spain and can be emulated by India and other developing countries. National interest has to be given priority over international agreement.

Accordingly, India's National Action Plan on Climate Change (NAPCC) unveiled in 2008, stuck to three points, viz. (i) India's per capita GHG's emission would at no point exceed that of the developed countries, (ii) India would not commit to specific emission reduction targets or energy efficiency targets, and (iii) India's plan would be implemented through eight missions such as: (a) enhancing solar energy contribution to total energy mix, (b) introducing energy efficiency steps, (c) promoting sustainable habitats, (d) saving Himalayan glaciers, (e) water resources management, (f) protecting mountain eco-systems, (g) improving eco-system services, and (h) making agriculture more resilient and adaptable to climate change. These are expected to meet our growth objectives through ecologically sustainable path and would increase our bargaining power at international discussion. The proposals without specific targets may not convince developed countries. We have to specify the targets. We produce nuclear energy to the extent of 3 percent of total energy. If we can install 2,00,000 MW of nuclear power by 2020 it would save the world 145 million tones of carbon emission. Our wind energy potential is assessed 45,000 MW; now we generate only 7,200 MW. [11]

Whether it is global warming or broader scenario of ecological imbalance, it is due to the lifestyle we have adopted. This lifestyle consumes much modern gadgets which causes irreparable damage to the nature. Fred Pearce in his book "Confessions of an Eco-sinner: Travels to Find Where Myself Comes From", gives an exhaustive account of how use of gold, prawn, cotton, mobile phones destroy huge area of rocks, land, forest and the course of nature. A Government sponsored study in Sweden says that only 1/10th of the world's population can be supported at the standard prevailing in Sweden. A Human Development Report says, "if the pattern of living in North is replicated in South it will require 10 times the present fossil fuel and 200 times the mineral wealth. Such a goal is infeasible and dangerous". [12]

Steps Taken By Some Countries

Denmark which derives 80 percent of its energy from fossil fuels appointed a committee to study the feasibility for a fossil-free country in 40 years. Germany funded 47 billion Euros in subsidies in solar energy but produces 0.1 percent of total energy supply. Denmark took step for wind energy but the result is not inspiring. Massive effort is required to transmit energy from sun and wind areas to the place of use. Scientists say, there are huge deposits of coal which will be used for hundreds of years and with new cracking technology, gas can be significantly boosted by conventional sources like tar and sands. Cost of eliminating fossil fuels have to be substantial i.e. 5 percent of GDP per year. Prioritizing research on green energy is an immediate need.

Realising the significance of the study of ecology, the United Nations recently brought out a report. The Economics of Ecosystems and Biodiversities has drawn our attention to the wanton desecration of the environment. The Report has made the profound statements that the value of nature and its services is worth trillions of dollars. Forests, fresh water, soils and coral reefs are enormously valuable. The value of coral reefs has been estimated at between US$ 3 billion and US$ 17.3 billion. Its destruction can harm marine life, and damage reef-based resource for food production. The value of the damage has been placed between US$ 2 trillion and US$ 4.5 trillion annually. The report is relevant in the context of India's Niyam Giri Hills, Noida, Nayachar and Posco Plant in Orissa.

The developed countries are to reduce 80 percent carbon emission by 2050. To restrict the global temperature to below 2 degree celsius as per the Copenhagen Accord, needs stress on equity, per capita carbon emission, shift of policy to a new green revolution and tax trade policy considering the country obligation to reduce carbon emission. [13]

The Intergovernmental Panel on Climate Change (IPCC) fears that global temperature will rise between 1.5 and 2.5 degree Celsius by 2050 with an estimated rise of 1.5 to 5.8 degree Celsius by 2100. The dreaded rise in sea level will mean that brackish water will encroach cultural land.

Energy use may be reduced by raising the cost of energy. But this will force us out of global market and threatens our economic survival. Increased production of energy leads us to environmental trap. A way out of this dilemma is to improve energy efficiency. The use of CFL lamps instead of bulbs, can lead to huge saving of energy. The use of hybrid cars can save petrol. Better insulation in buildings can save energy used in conditioning. Wind and solar energy are more environmental friendly than thermal, nuclear and hydro, but they create indicative waste or destroy riverine culture. But there is a limit to the production of this energy. Hence, to protect the environment and survival of our civilization, the alternative is to reduce the use of energy.

The International Geosphere Biosphere Programme of 2008 drew vision for 2050 which identified the global goal as improvement in human well-being in line with sustainable development with a new model where consumers considered their needs rather than their wants. Decoupling energy use from economic growth requires a model shift in transport pattern modifying the nature of urbanisation process and land use that puts stress on natural resources. Policy framework tailored to social value creation needs to be developed.

Almost all countries of the world feel deeply concerned about the climate change and meet at various conventions to think of measures to check climate deterioration.

Following Kyoto, at Cancun, the UN climate conference in December 2010 reached a compromise to set up US$ 100 billion 'Green Fund' to fight global warming. But there was no agreement on extending the landmark Kyoto Protocol on emission cuts beyond 2012. The Convenion decided to promote efforts in poor nations to protect their climate-friendly tropical forests with the prospect of financial compensation from richer nations. The agreement to cut developed country-emission by 25-40 percent by 2020 without any concrete mechanism to achieve the goal stands in the company of sentiment if not at sanctimony.

End Notes

1. Depak Basu, Warming the Earth, The Statesman, April 6, 2010.
2. D.N. Bose, Earth and the World, Statesman, 21 February, 2010.
3. Chandanthel P. Geevan, Copenhagen, Accountability is Vital, Economic Times, December 1, 2009.
4. Soma Bajerjee, Why Should We Pay for Big Emitters?, Economic Times, 30 November, 2009.
5. M. Raz-Hasn, 'Jaw-Jaw in Copenhagen', The Statesman, 5 December, 2009.
6. Swaminathan, S. Anklesaria an Aiyar, Carbon Cuts: Penalty or

Insurance?, Economic Times, December 9, 2009.

7.   Bjorn Lamberg, Climate Change and Climate Gate, Economic Times, December, 2009.

8.   Deepak Basu, Op. cit.

9.   Bjorn Lomberg, Taking Sense on Global Warming, Economic Times, 17 May, 2010.

10.   Bjorn Lomborg, Cars Bombs and Climate Change, Economic Times, December, 2010.

11.   P.P. Sangal, India's Climate Change Action Plan, Economic Times, 2008.

12.   Bharat Dogra, Lifestyle and Ecology. The Statesman, 7 July, 2008.

13.   Mukul Sanwat, Climate Policy Needs a Basic Shift, Economic Times, 13 January, 2010.

19

Economic Development and the Elements of Nature

'Nature teaches beasts to know their friend's
One touch of nature makes the whole world kin.'
- Shakespeare

The above profound observations of Shakespeare open our eyes at present when, we lying in the lap of nature, tighten our embrace and squeeze blood from her breasts. In a time when we realize the hard truth in Gandhi's wise statement, "the Earth provides enough to satisfy every man's means but not every man's greed". We have to soberly think of the relationship between the nature and the modern economic development and mend our ways to restore and retain healthy relation between man and nature. It is no exaggeration that modern science has enabled mankind to subjugate and exploit the nature to satisfy his endless greed and in consequence the nature as if in vengeance has wrought disaster on man's life and threatens with grim future.

Rapid industrialization, profuse use of energy, mechanization of production, increasing population, globalization and consumerism in its train have put unbearable pressure on the natures' elements—air, sunshine, water, land and vegetation. Mankind suffers not only due the scarcity of the nature's gift, but also due to the pollution of air, water and soil. The relative importance of these three elements is obvious from the fact that we cannot live for more than 4 to 5 minutes without air, nor can we live for more than 4 to 5 days without water. No plant can grow without soil. On an average, a person requires 0.6 kg. of food, 1.4 kg. of water and 13.5 kg. of air per day. Realisation of this has led to the extensive and intensive study of the change taking place in the state of natural elements and set to think of remedial measures. In this write up we would discuss the problems faced by mankind owing to the change occurring in the conditions of water, air and soil.

Water: The Life Blood of the Animal World

It is common knowledge that water is required for multifarious purposes, mostly for drinking and cleaning, cultivating land and producing industrial goods. Water transport is also essential for trade and human movement.

Most early civilizations developed around fresh water which was essential for consumption, agriculture, commerce transport, defence and other uses. Water is an essential variable of economic development. Unfortunately, India's per capita availability of water has declined from 2309 cu in 1991 to below 1700 cu at present. If we do not change our ways dramatically, our per capita water availability would be about 1000 cu by 2050.

Rainfall is the chief source of water in India. We receive 4000 billion cubic metres annually. About 85 percent of rainfall is confined to 4-5 months of the year and varies widely from just 300 mm in the western belt to a massive 10400 mm in Meghalaya. This uneven rainfall causes both flood and drought.

We have no storage capacity to capture the rainfall. The developed countries capture and store over 500 days of rainfall in major river basins; India captures just 30 days. Of the total precipitation, a mere 1,123 bcm of water is available for utilization, 690 bcm in the shape of surface water and 433 bcm as ground water resource. While supply of water is finite, demand is growing; our agriculture uses 85 percent of the water supplies, industry uses 5 percent and domestic consumption 6 percent.

There is excessive unregulated drawing of ground water leading to continuous depletion as there is little effort to recharge it. Each consuming sector poses specific challenge. In agriculture, crop selection is perverse with water-stressed areas growing water-intensive crops like rice, wheat and sugarcane. Production of 1 kg. of rice requires 3000 litres of water and water-saving agricultural technology is not reaching a large number of fragmented farmers.

Our industry consumes 8 percent of total water. Of the total industrial consumption of water, 88 percent is accounted for by thermal power use. Only 60 percent of the waste water generated by industry is treated.

The efficiency of water supply by municipalities in urban areas is less than 50 percent with water leaks being illegally tapped. In rural areas, people have no access to clean drinking water.

Nelson Mandela in 2002 at the World Summit on Sustainable Development in Johannesburg said. "One of the many things I learned as president was the centrality of water in the social, political and economic affairs of the country, the continent and the world. Water sits at the nexus of food security, education, gender empowerment and global disease". [1]

Challenge to Protect the Valuable Resources

The US facing water problem in 1960s raised the efficiency of water use. It resulted in per capita water consumption dropping by 20 percent between 1980 and 2000. Singapore has been able to reuse 100 percent of their waste water and to recycle 10 percent of the entire waste water.

In India too, there are many organizations conserving and recycling waste water. We need to leverage technology, innovation, investments, collaboration and new learning to solve the burning issues.

It is found in the studies that embankments constructed for generation of hydro-electricity and irrigation create enormous green house gases. Eric Duchemin says that the embankment creates carbon dioxide and methane. The plants submerged in water reservoir produce methane. Lands covered by embankments in some countries are as follows: Russia-79.6 lakh hectares, Canada-65 lakh hectares, US-69.6 lakh hectares, India-45.7 lakh hectares, Brazil-39.8 lakh hectares, China-58 lakh hectares.

Water pollution is a serious problem. In the state of Orissa, 90 percent of people are deprived of pure drinking water. In 24 districts, underground water level is going down. In the world, demand for water for various uses is steadily increasing while supply is gradually shrinking.

In the entire world, the amount of water available is 1.4 billion cubic km. with only 2.5 percent of the available water being sweet and 69 percent of this sweet water is in the form of ice, 20 percent as under ground and 1 percent on the surface of the Earth. Sweet water amounts to 36 million cubic km. of which 28 cubic km. is covered by ice. Only 8 million cubic km. is available underground in the rivers and lakes.

In the world, 110 crore people are not getting sufficient water, 250 crore are deprived of clean water and by 2025, 280 crore people in 48 countries will face water shortage. The number will reach 400 crore by 2050. The IPCC scientists observed in 1996 that availability of water per capita has come down to 1000 cm. Now, Jordan, Israel, Somalia, Algeria and Kenya are having minimum quantity of water. Similar situation will occur in Libya, South Africa, Iran and Ethiopia, within 20 to 30 years.

Conflict arises between countries over the use of river water. In our country conflict arises on water use between states. Big companies are taking lease of water areas and selling water to people—conflict arises over the use of water by agriculture or industry and who should be given the priority in use of water. Delivering the Nalco Foundation Day Lecture at Angul, Orissa, Dr. R.K.C. Pachauri said that the world will be in dire situation as far as water stress is concerned. Africa will be the worst hit and parts of India too will be partially affected by 2025. Over three million people will be living in water stress hit countries.

Agriculture will be impacted. There is 5 to 10 percent drop in yield for every degree of rise in temperature. By the year 2015, there will be a 30 percent reduction in yield in Central and South Asia and by 2020 there will be a 50 percent drop in yield in Africa. The sea level rise due to thermal expansion as well as melt down of glaciers is to the order of 17 cm. In the 20th century, the cyclones have dropped in terms of frequency but have increased manifold in terms of their intensity; drought and flood frequency too has increased.

India is fortunate to have enough water resources, but it is not evenly distributed between the states. Orissa is a state replete with rivers and lakes. Its water resources can be used up to 75 percent. It is envisioned that by 2050, the rivers inside the state will have constant water flows, but water available from neighbouring states will decline from 37,556 bcm to 25,272 bcm. According to a 2001 estimate, underground water in the state may be put to use to the extent of 21,011 bcm of which 68 percent can be used without danger. In Orissa, in 2001, the average per capita water was 3,359 cum against India's average of 1,820 cum. But by 2054, it will be 2,218 cum due to population increase. Orissa government formulated a water policy in 2007 keeping in view the Indian government's water policy of 2002. Our lifestyle, economic policy, agricultural pattern etc. have to be changed in line with change in water resources.

The problem of pollution of underground water is being aggravated gradually. The central underground water organization surveying 1100 tube wells found that in 8.5 percent of the wells, there is excessive floride. According to the WHO, iron content in water from 0.3 m to 1 m is not harmful. In Orissa, in places like Patkura Pichakuli, Astarang and Parjang, iron contents in tube well water varies from 6.5 m to 9.2 m. In cromite areas, excessive cromite content in water is found. Nitrate in water from 45 n to 100 n, is not harmful.

Industrial use of water constitutes 7-8 percent of total water consumption. However, 1 litre of discharged water pollutes 7 to 8 litres of water. Hence, industries account for 30-50 percent of water used in our country.

Land Use, Soil Erosion and Degradation

Mega projects and big industries are having increasing claim on land and this diverts land, even fertile land from agriculture to non-agricultural activities. This has happened world over and in our country too.

Taking the case of Orissa, the state government has signed 47 MoUs with companies to set up steel plants. Tata Steel Plant at Kalinga Nagar will displace 1,100 families, POSCO is to construct a steel plant at Paradeep to produce 12 million tons of steel. This requires 4004.25 acres of land of which 2951.56 acres is forest land. Arcelor Mittal has decided to set up a steel plant at Keonjhar to produce 12 million tons of steel which requires 8000 acres of land. ESSAR Steel at Paradeep needs 2500 acres of land, Jindal Steel and Power will set up a 7 million tonne capacity steel plant at Angul for which it requires 5750 acres of land. It has already acquired 3000 acres of land. Bhusan Steel Plant to produce 3 million tons of steel needs 2000 acres of land of which 1800 acres have been acquired.

The government of Orissa has also agreed to give POSCO 3000 acres of land to construct a port at Jatadhari. It has also given a lease of 6240 hectares of land for mining to POSCO in Keonjhar and Sundergarh districts. Orissa Mining Corporation is getting about ₹ 3,000 per ton of iron ore from POSCO and the government will get only ₹ 26 per ton. For 30 years, POSCO needs 600 million tons of iron ore, but it is taking lease to raise 1000 million tons. [2] Confronted with the problem of land acquisition, the Central government has taken steps to amend Land Acquisition Act of 1894 through the Rehabilitation and Resettlement Bill which has not yet been passed by the Parliament.

No convincing answers are yet available to three crucial questions: (i) How much and what kind of land could be acquired now and in future? (ii) will ruthless acquisition of arable land jeopardise food security? (iii) will acquisition further reduce the country's forest cover already far below the National Forest Policy target of one third of the geographical area?

The first legal move to acquire land for public purpose was the promulgation and regulation of 1824 Bengal Code. The first Land Acquisition Act was passed in 1870 which was replaced by the 1894 Act which applies to the whole country. The Act provided for no-opinion of the affected persons.

The 1894 Act did not exempt land tilled by tribals from acquisition. Out of nearly 60 million owners and tillers, displaced by acquisitions between 1954 and 2004, about one-fifth belonged to scheduled tribes. The Centre admits that only 28 percent of them have been rehabilitated. The Bill on the anvil should incorporate the relevant sections of the Panchayat (Extension to Scheduled Areas) Act, 1996 and of the Scheduled Tribes and Other Traditional Forest-Dwellers (Recognition of Forest Rights) Act, 2007. Under these Acts, the government has restored to the tribal population, the ownership, collection, processing, trade and marketing of minor forest products. In 1997, the Supreme Court also ruled out the acquisition of tribal land and forests.

The Bill should address the core recommendations of the 2007 National Rehabilitation Policy under which both acquisition and displacement should be minimum. Selection of the land to be acquired should not be left to the discretion of the scrutiny committee, as in the draft Bill, but made statutory.

No acquisition bill or amendments provided for the return of acquired land if it was not used or acquired in excess. This was the main demand of the opposition's movement in Singur. The Supreme Court has also ruled that land acquired in the public interest has to be used for that purpose only, if it is not, it has to be used for some other purpose of public interest, failing which the land has to be auctioned and proceeds used for public utility. Tamil Nadu has enacted legislation for the return of unused acquired land to the original owners. The Land Acquisition Bill should set a time-limit for the utilization of acquired land. Highly fertile multi-crop land should be out of bounds from acquisition in order to preserve food security. [3] Public complaints forced the UPA government to draft a new bill.

The R & R Bill envisages compensation at the rate of 90 percent of the market value, or the floor area rate (whichever is higher) for normal acquisition and 75 percent of the same for urgent acquisition. It has proposed a Land Acquisition Disputes Settlement Authority for each State, which the affected owners can approach. Besides allotment of land in lieu of the acquired land to the extent possible, the Bill recommends employment of at least one person from each affected family. When land is acquired, the owner not only loses it forever but also misses recurrent income from crops, seeds and by-products. Acquisition should, therefore, provide for a recurrent income to the owners, either lumpsum or in the form of free shares, if an industry is built upon it by the government or a private company.

No acquisition law ever provided for compensating the loss of common property like pastures and forest waste land etc. The bone of contention is the acquiring authority. The Bill envisages that if a private company buys 70 percent of its requirement directly from owners, the government can acquire the remaining 30 percent. The left wants quid pro quo in such deeds. The Bill provides for acquisition for joint venture.

Excavation of minerals on hilly regions causes immense damage to forest resource and water streams essential to people's living in down slope. Gandhmardan Mountains contains biggest bauxite deposit in Asia under its 10 km, long and 2 km. wide belt. In its 230 million tons bauxite deposit, there are 45-75 percent of alumina oxide and 2.23 percent of silicon. Orissa has 13 bauxite mines out of which 6 have been leased out. Gandhamardan Mountains are famous not only for stones, streams and plants but also for great epics, history, archaeology, religion, philosophy and tourism.

The famous temples of Nrusinghnath (1413) Srihari Sankar are abodes of Bishnu and Shiva. This mountain is a place of congregation of Aryan, Dravidian vaishnovite and sakta cults. The mountain has more than 3,000 medicinal plants as per British scientist H.N. Hirics (1921-23). Botanical Survey of India in 1963-64, led by Gopinath Panigrahi and Hirbat Muni (1950) located 2,400 medicinal plants; in 1994-95, M. Brahma and Hariom Saksena detected 714 medicinal plants in the mountain. R.C. Mishra on behalf of Regional Plant Resources Centre of Bhubaneswar has described in detail the various medicinal plants existing on the mountain in his survey report. Apprehending the loss of these rich plants and heritage, people vehemently protested against leasing for bauxite mines on this hill to Vedanta Company.

Health of the soil is the basis for the health of the plants that grow on it. It is the soil of the surface and the soil found at about 15-20 centimetres depth which is important. The top soil is not lifeless. There are scores of living active microbes in each cubic centimetre of fertile topsoil. The living and life-giving soil is poisoned by the folly of man. Application of excessive chemical, fertilizer and pesticide and industrial effluents are continuously polluting the soil. Mining activities of all kinds destroy the landscape and contaminate soil. Besides soil pollution, there occurs soil degradation, salination and soil erosion. Soil erosion due to water and wind, increased salinity due to insufficient drainage, soil erosion due to faulty cultivation practice, destruction of forests overgrazing etc, create great concern and remind us what US President said long back, "a nation which destroys its soil destroys itself". [4]

Air Pollution: A Grave Danger

It is true that nature displays its mood through its elements particularly air, followed by water, rain, flood etc. Shakespeare wondered, "how sometimes nature will betray its folly. Its tenderness, make itself a pastime, to harder bosoms". Our behaviour in modern age adds to the folly of nature and spoil its elements. We have in preceding pages discussed how water and soil got spoiled thanks to our carelessness that inflicts misery on mankind. Air we inhale and wind we play with sometimes become cruel to us and for this we have to blame ourselves to a great extent.

Pollution is the price that mankind has to pay for indiscriminate growth. Air is the precious element of nature that is in the atmosphere enveloping the Earth. 78 percent of the atmospheric gases is nitrogen and 21 percent is oxygen. What we want for bodily requirement is oxygen. This is found in the portion of atmosphere closer to Earth.

Pollution of air is caused by nature itself as well as by men putting huge wastes and chemicals into atmosphere. Natural phenomena like volcanic eruption, cyclone, forest fire emitting several gases cause air pollution. Historically, atmospheric pollution began with the invention of fire and got aggravated by discovery of coal, invention of steam engine and rise in automobiles.

The atmospheric pollution does not respect political boundaries. The effect of pollution spreads faraway from its source. The sources of pollutant are industries, power plants, automobiles, pesticides, forest fires, agricultural waste, kitchen smokes etc. The atomic power plants emit hazardous radioactive substances in the atmosphere. Number of automobiles in the world increased from 50 million in 1950 to 530 million in 2002. Burning fossil fuels (coal, oil gas) is the most important atmospheric pollution.

The consequence of atmospheric pollution is far-reaching. It exerts undesirable impact on clouds, temperature and precipitation.

Air pollution is dangerous to human health. Carbon dioxide is poisonous to humans and sulphur dioxide attacks the lungs.

Metropolitan cities suffer most from atmospheric pollution. The problem of Beijing is the presence of high level of sulphur dioxide. There is high concentration of lead in the cities of Karachi and Cairo, Los Angeles and Tokyo which face concentration of ozone at the ground level. Mumbai experiences more asthma than other cities. The incident of cancer in Delhi, Mumbai, Chennai and Bengaluru is double that of rural areas.

Solution to the industrial pollution is found in the adoption of new technology which is evaded for fear of profit reduction. Substitute of fossil fuels is to be found in non-conventional sources of energy like solar and wind. Transport policy should be geared to encourage public transport. Cycle use may be encouraged as in Holland by constructing separate lines. Green manure has to be used more and more.

Measures to Check Environmental Degradation

Quite aware of the imminent danger of the neglect of the environment in pursuit of economic development, government has formulated a policy to maintain and promote environmental excellence.

The MoEF has brought about the new EIA Notification with effect from 14th September, 2006. The notification makes it mandatory for various projects such as mining, the small power plants, river valley, infrastructure, ports, roads, highways, harbours and airports and industrial units to get environmental clearance. Unlike the EIA Notification of 1999, the new legislation has put the onus of clearing projects on the State Level Impact Assessment Authority depending on the size capacity of the project. The notification states that construction of projects or expansion or modernization of existing project shall be undertaken after prior environmental clearance from the Central government or as the case may be through State Level assessment body. For all projects under 'A' category, public consultation has been made mandatory.

A comparative study of advantage and disadvantage of a project from different angles, environmental, economic and social would go a long way in determining its desirability and acceptability by the area people. The knottiest problem is displacement and rehabilitation. Compensation for the land acquired is often not agreeable to the parties concerned. Explaining and convincing the people of the utility of the project is a time taking sincere and intelligent effort which in most cases is not properly discharged. That is why severe disputes and agitations have come up in some cases right from the initial phase of undertaking the projects such as steel projects at Kalinga Nagar, and car project in West Bengal. Signing MoU with the foreign and Indian companies by the state Governments in hot haste have been the root cause of troubles arising later. Our anxiety to usher in rapid economic development without consideration of long-term effects is not rational.

The challenge is to resolve conflicting requirements— rapid economic growth on the one hand and balancing it with sustainable use of natural resources given the rising population, fragility of natural resources and low subsistence level of majority of people on the other hand. Pachauri says, "we have exceeded the capacity of the Earth by 25 percent and this has been so over the last two decades".

Considering the imminent danger, every drop of water must be used judiciously, every building should be designed as a green building with least minimum consumption and emission, the dependence has to shift from private transport to public transport and renewable energy put to optimum use, be it wind or solar or any other.

End Notes

1. Sanjeev Chadha, Water-The Country's Inconvenient Truth, Economic Times, 30th August, 2010.
2. Dharitree, 15th November, 2010.
3. Bibeknand Roy, Good Earth up for Grabs, Economic Times, 24th November 2009.
4. Gopinathan Nair, Earth in Peril, Publication Division, Government of India, 2005, p. 3.

20

Challenges of Globalization

The impact of globalization taking a stride since the last two decades has been a mixed one—some countries and some sections of a particular country benefiting highly while some others are either growing slowly or sliding down. Globalization accompanied by liberalization and loosening of state control has no doubt widened the space of competition, given incentive to innovation that has raised efficiency and productivity resulting in rapid growth of the economy. The salubrious effect of globalization-led growth has, of course been shrouded by problems like inequality, increasing marginalization, displacement, joblessness and ecological disaster. The problems are not insoluble but require careful monitoring which often does not take place either due to incompetence of the rulers and administrators or policy bias towards the privileged. The concept of 'inclusive growth' has been woven around the requirements that would mitigate the evil effects of globalization and pave the way for growth with equity.

Here an attempt is made to: (i) decipher the meaning of 'inclusive growth' pointing out its constituents, (ii) assess the steps taken sofar in our country to promote inclusive growth, and (iii) analyze the lacunae and suggest remedies.

The Eleventh Five Year Plan of India defines inclusive growth as 'the growth process which yields broad-based benefits and ensures equality of opportunity for all'. The Plan was designed to reduce poverty and focus on bridging the various divides that continue to fragment our society. It is heartening that the growth rate of the Indian economy has accelerated from about 5.6 percent in 1980s to 8 percent in 1990s and to 9 percent in the first decade of the present century. The benefits of growth have not accrued equitably to all sections of the people and to all regions. To realize the objectives of inclusive growth, some policy intervention was made in the Eleventh Plan and some success was achieved. In the Twelfth Five Year Plan (2012-2017), greater emphasis has been given on the goal of inclusive and faster growth. For the purpose, the Planning Commission has identified twelve issues for discussion and suggestion which may be compressed in to four broad themes such as: (i) enhancing human resources for inclusive growth, employment and welfare, (ii) sustainable growth and transformation, (iii) market reforms for efficiency and inclusiveness, and (iv) governance reforms through decentralization.

Areas to be developed for inclusive growth appear to be micro, small and medium enterprises and agriculture and tourism which are likely to generate huge multiplier impact.

The sole purpose is to provide all able-bodied people an opportunity to earn a minimum income for having a decent and happy life. Of course, the concept of happiness is changing. With recent depression and slow down in the Western economies, there has been an urge to shed obsession with increase in GDP as a measure of happiness. The French president Nicolas Sarkozy asked other nations to adopt measures of well-being in the metric of progress. Prime Minister David Cameron of UK asked the office of National Statistics to produce an index to gauge the general well-being of the people by assessing their psychological and environmental well-being. Krueger, Kahneman and their colleagues while developing National Time Accounting as against National Income Accounting based on enjoyment feeling found that very low income caused bad mood and high income was associated with higher tensions. On this finding, they conclude that the link between income and happiness is exaggerated. In 1970, economist Richerd Easterin observed that economic growth did not lead to more happiness over time. In 2007, Pew Global Attitude Survey found little link between GDP of countries and the self reported levels of happiness of their residents. [1]

Economist Angus Deaton's research shows that life satisfaction increases with per capita GDP when GDP increases proportionately rather than in absolute terms. Of course self reported happiness and satisfaction do not reveal the quality of life. Yet, obsession with GDP growth creates an illusion.

Growth is nonetheless imperative for poverty eradication and redistribution. How much improvement in the condition of the poor will be possible only if redistributive measures are taken when as in 2004-2005 our per-capita consumption was only ₹ 725 per month at current prices? Land redistributed by 1990 accounted for only 1.25 percent of total land. Redistributive measures hardly trickle down to the targeted people—only 10 percent of food subsidy actually reaches the poor. MGNREGA''s case is same. Hence, redistribution without growth is meaningless. [2]

, The key to inclusive growth lies in policies that stimulate growth in jobs. The basic requirement of job creation is spread of education that would widen outlook, give skills and high level of technology for the growth. The recent NSSO statistics say that in the last five years unemployment has declined. They also indicate that growth of employment has declined too. Unemployment has declined because young boys and girls are going in for education and employment has declined because jobs are not created adequately.

While providing various types of education to an increasing number of youth, efforts have to be made to develop sectors/areas wherein job opportunities are maximum. Young people's skills and aspirations have to be aligned with requisite jobs. India's labour force is expected to increase by 32 percent in the next 20 years. Hence, 250 million additional jobs must be created by that much time. Agriculture is no doubt the greatest provider of jobs, but its expansion is saddled with many problems. Manufacturing has been recognized as a huge and so far missed opportunity. Plans being developed by the government aim to grow 100 million jobs by 2025. Further, services requiring various levels of skills would also provide jobs.

This requires spread of education of right type. The University Grants Commission (UGC) enrolment data shows that actual enrolment has increased from 6.65 million in 2000-01 to 13-64 million in 2008-09. Yet, the number is not sufficient to ensure a smooth transition of labour from agriculture to manufacturing and services. The higher education system in its present structure and content is ill-suited to meet the desired skill requirements of the millions; particularly in the country side the higher institutions are not equitably distributed and the quality of studies does not match. The school education in India is in a pathetic state with only 53 percent of children in standard V in rural India who can read a standard II level text and only 36 percent of students in standard V who can do a simple division. NCAER study shows that 50 percent of the students dropout after class X. Government does not bother about the problems in middle and secondary levels. The number of individuals in the age group of 20-24 going to college in our country is only 13 percent as against 23 percent in China. Hence, it is imperative to strengthen the base of our educational system and improve the quality.

Agriculture

With slow growth and increasing instability and inter-region disparities, agricultural sector poses both problems and prospects for inclusive growth. Agriculture has lost its attractiveness with relatively low-earning thanks to low productivity and marketing hurdles. From 2001-02 to 2003-06, yield level of food grains remained almost stagnant at 0.5 percent growth rate. In this period, while rice yield growth had shown fluctuation, wheat recorded a negative growth. Inter-regional disparity (across 17 major states) in agricultural GDP growth calculated in terms of co-efficient of variations increased from 50 percent during the period 1983-84 to 1993-94 to 103 percent during the period 1993-94 to 2003-2004. The public investment in agriculture continues to be at a very low level. Private investment has not met the deficiency in public investment. The share of agriculture in the total Gross Capital Formation (GCF) (at 1999-2000 prices) was only 7.7 percent in 2005-06. There has been a decline in large holdings both in number and operational area concentration at the bottom has increased. The small and marginal farms taken together constitute about 82 percent of holdings and more than 39 percent of operational areas. [3]

Can we protect the small holders and eliminate poverty? Green Revolution was confined to a few states and crops. Now that also has shown fatigue. Technology used in dry lands has not made much head way. Further, cultivable lands are getting transferred from the tillers due to industrialization, urbanization and housing.

Agricultural sector has two sections of people, one farmers and the other farm labourers. The well-being of the agricultural labourers is reflected by their wages. From the Shimla data of Agricultural Ministry it was found that farm wages from January 2008 to December 2010 shot up 108.5 percent in Andhra Pradesh, 84.4 percent in Punjab, 74.7 percent in Haryana, 73.6 percent in Tamilnadu, 58.3 percent in Bihar, 56.3 percent in Madhya Pradesh, 62.8 percent in Orissa and 62.3 percent in Uttar Pradesh. Thus, there is an enormous improvement even allowing for 38-33 percent inflation in this period. However, it has not translated itself into poverty fall perhaps because of poor monsoon in 2009.

Infrastructure

Our country is now in a dilemma—monetary policy, interest rate hike to check inflation that is at about 9 percent may stifle demand which may affect growth. Fiscal consolidation is an imperative, but we cannot compromise on capital expenditure while we persist with revenue spending like subsides. If we do not want GDP growth to slow down, reduction in demand to check inflation should be matched by increase in investment i.e. C+I+G. This heightens the need for infrastructure building. [4]

Now that US and European economies are facing slow down, the emerging economies of Asia are to look to themselves for growth. During 2003-2007, the share of the emerging economies in the world GDP rose from 20 percent to 34 percent. The growth rate of these economies which averaged 7 percent in 2003-2007 is likely to slump down to 5 percent. In the 1990s, global growth averaged 2.9 percent, powered mainly by US before spiking to 4.7 percent from 2003 to 2007 powered mainly by the big emerging markets. [5]

But the momentum of growth and inclusiveness of the growth process very much depends on infrastructural growth in emerging economies including India. The Commission on Growth and Development constituted by the World Bank has opined that infrastructure spending is very much neglected in the growing Asian countries and public investment in these countries works out to 5-7 percent of GDP (The World Bank, 2008). A composite index of infrastructure development among 17 major states in India worked out for the year 2004-05 reveals wide disparity with Kerala securing top rank (0.6322) and Assam remaining at the bottom (0.1353). [6] Unless and until all regions of the country have well-developed infrastructure, the potential of production and marketing cannot be adequately developed to facilitate inclusive growth.

Tourism

Tourism is another sector which has great potential for creating jobs. India has enormous wealth of attraction, natural, cultural and historical for the tourists which needs to be exploited. Tourism creates jobs with less capital investment—

78 jobs per million rupees compared to 45 jobs per million rupees in manufacturing sector. It provides employment to wide spectrum of job seekers from the unskilled to the specialized. Employment ramification of tourism comprises various types of workers and women, urban and rural, traders and hoteliers. Internationally, women account for 70 percent of work force in the tourism industry. Globally, tourism is a critical economic sector employing 250 million people—8 percent of global employment, accounting for 9 percent of the world's GDP and 9 percent of the global investment. In India, tourism is expected to generate 37 million additional jobs in the next 10 years.

In the last decade there has occurred a three-fold increase in domestic tourist arrivals to approximately 650 million and over a two-fold increase in foreign tourist arrivals to 5.6 million. Yet, our potential has not been fully exploited. As stated in a recent Travel and Tourism Competitiveness Report by the World Economic Forum, the key challenges are lack of: (a) quality infrastructure, (b) skill development, (c) conducive policy framework, and (d) coordination among various authorities. [7] To address effectively these challenges a three-pronged approach has to be made, including: (i) adopting a PPP model to address infrastructure constraints as in Karnataka, Kerala and Andhra Pradesh. This approach would make larger projects as integrated town destinations, eco-tourism, medical tourism, adventure tourism and golf tourism. A special purpose vehicle or a co-operative may be formed with equity from promoters, private investors and local community, (ii) conducive policy framework for tourism development involving implementing institutional framework that leads to synergistic development by coordinated participation from multiple authorities, (iii) leveraging technology—online travel industry has made travelling more convenient. Its scope has to be expanded pan India with travel currency cards, online travel and hotel booking, timely information exchange between stake holders etc.

Sustainable Growth

The trade-off between environment and development drew the attention of the world leaders at the Stockholm Conference on the Human Development in 1972. As at that time, the overriding consideration was poverty eradication. Developing economies like India and China attached less importance to environment than to development and industrialization. Industrialization and urbanization are essential elements of economic growth. From the experience of US, Europe and China, it is understood that once a saturation level is achieved, the nature of pollution and environmental damage it causes, changes.

A country has to resolve the trade off at this stage of economic growth. China is expected to reach this level in regard to infrastructure, appliances and building in 2030-40. Resources in construction materials, and minerals and ores rose 34 and 27 times respectively and oil use increased 12 times and biomass by only 3.8 times. In India, about 50 crore of people are expected to move to towns by 2020. Infrastructure building for them poses a big challenge—we do not know how the resulting degradation and increased emission originating from massive production of infrastructure materials electricity etc. be accommodated in transition to sustainable development.

Sustainable development implies optimum use of natural resources with minimum ecological effect. It means finding out renewable source of energy and building materials that can keep up the level of development for long future.

We need to have a clearly defined sustainable development framework for mining, infrastructure and urbanization. The three pillars of sustainable development comprise: (i) development of new knowledge of the interconnection of environmental, economic, and social system, (ii) establishment of performance indicators, metrics and public reporting, (iii) the continuing well-being of the local population. [8] Finally, transformation to sustainability requires modifying demand and the lifestyles of the rich and restricting exports of natural resources.

Institutional Bottlenecks to be Removed!

A key element in the strategy of inclusive growth is an all-out effort to develop a process which would ensure that the development fund injected for a programme must be utilized for the population for whom it is meant, with least leakage. The delivery process must ensure timely delivery.

The Committee on Financial Inclusion and the Committee on Financial Sector Reforms stressed better financial inclusion. The commercial banks have extended the scope of banking to the weaker sections through introduction of no-frills account. But the achievement is quite dismal. The NSSO Survey, 2003 reveals that of the total indebted farmer households, 56 percent obtained loans from formal sources and 44 percent from informal sources. The share of direct accounts with a credit limit of less than ₹ 25,000 in total direct accounts has declined from 97 percent in 1990 to 67 percent in 2005. Rural branches of commercial banks declined from 35,389 in 1993 to 32,108 in 2005 (RBI, 2004-05) Thus, there is a gap between intention and reality in respect of financial inclusion.

Microfinance organizations in recent years have done appreciable work in some countries to provide finance to the poor. If properly regulated and linked with commercial banks, they can render much greater financial service to the poor of our country.

Reforms in Governance

Reforms in governance is essential for inclusive growth. For facilitating decision by the concerned people and implementing projects by local people, decentralization of administration has to take place. Panchayati Raj is meant for people's participation in their own welfare programmes. But it is noticed that there has not been serious efforts to transfer resources and responsibilities to local bodies.

Governance of a country operates at various stages from ministry to local officers. For efficacy, there must be a regular transmission of inputs from the top to bottom layers of governance. Similarly, there must be constant feedback from the bottom to the top and this be analyzed with due diligence.

There should be concurrent monitoring and evaluation of programme once in a quarter. Appropriate success parameters should be laid down to adjudge success of a scheme.

The deprived sections of the people, schedule castes, tribes and women should be empowered and encouraged to take active part in Panchayati administration. The dominion of the MPs and MLAs in meetings of the Panchayat Samitis and Zilla Parishads has to be stopped. It is high time that subjects in the 11th and 12th schedules of the Constitution be transferred to the local bodies.

Institutional reforms must aim at motivating civil bureaucracy, local representatives and common people to do sincerely and efficiently what is desirable. [9]

Recent events manifest failed governance, systematic corruption engulfing the country and epitomizes people's disdain and alienation The Second Administrative Reform Commission acknowledged that governance is admittedly the, weak link in our quest for prosperity and equity. The steel frame is now a malleable and creaking bamboo frame.

The VIP culture is antithetical to and egalitarian democracy with its avowed good of equity and incisiveness. The civil servants should not seek post retirement appointment and political parties should restrain from putting pressure on top civil servants to do something for personal benefit. [10]

Concluding Remarks

Higher rate of growth and inclusive or widespread growth are not antithetical to each other. In a vast country benefiting larger number of people belonging to all sections of society, people require conscious and careful planning and sympathetic governance, sometimes checking the unfettered stride of the private sector. The key to inclusive growth lies in policies that encourage generation of more jobs and opportunities for salaried and self-employed. [11] Efficiency, competitiveness and cost-reduction are pre-requisites of inclusive growth. In our country, there are certain economic and social sectors which lend themselves to rapid and wider growth. From humanitarian point of view and thanks to the political compulsion in a democracy, some measures have to be taken to quickly help the poor and unprivileged sectors grow and conserve resources for the future generations. Considering all these and to sub-serve the interests of the people belonging to all sections and regions the following is suggested:

1. First and foremost our overriding aim should be to create as much more employment opportunities as possible
2. For the purpose of building up of infrastructure, road, transport, electricity, health, education and irrigation, social and economic infrastructure should get the top most priority.
3. Education with quality and utility has to be spread at subsidized rate or free to the children, particularly rural children. Educational reforms keeping in view the modern trend and applicability has to be undertaken from the primary stage. Skill formation and employability ought to be the primary goal.
4. Considering the evil impact of ecological deterioration and exhaustion of non-renewable resources, well thought out industrial development should take place.
5. Obsession with equality and craze for material consumption has to be checked. We observe increasing inequality in terms of the conditions of the people in poor states.
6. For providing more employment and earning opportunity sectors like agriculture, tourism small industries, service sector etc. have to be expanded.

Dreams will be realized only when honest, efficient, and foresighted selfless governance is manifest in all fields and all states.

End Notes

1. Neeraj Kaushal, Economics in Pursuit of Happiness, Economic Times, 23 June, 2011.
2. Arvind Pamgariya, Growth and Redistribution, Economic Times, 27 July, 2011
3. R.K. Panda, Inclusive growth in India-Recent Development and Challenges, Vision, Vol. XXIX, No. 1.
4. Aditya Puri, Spend Prudently-Build Infrastructure, Economic Times, 8 August, 2011.
5. Ruchir Sharma, The Third Coming of Emerging Economies, Economic Times, 8 August, 2011.
6. Kapil Anu and P.S. Raikhy, (2008), Role of Infrastructure in Economic Development of India-An Inter-state Analysis, The Indian Economic Association, 91st Conference Volume, Vol. 1.
7. Rana Kapour, Tourism and Inclusive India to Incredible India, Economic Times, 11 August, 2011.
8. Mukul Sanwal, No Growth Sans Hard Decisions, Economic Times, 15 Augsut, 2011.
9. Sanjib Chandra Hota, The Challenges of Inclusive Growth-A Case of Orissa, Vision, Vol. XXXI, No. 2-3.
10. Raghu Dayal, Wilt Thou, Mr. Prime Minister, Economic Times, 13 July, 2011.
11. Arun Maira, Keys to Inclusive Growth, Economic Times, 10 August, 2011.

Bibliography

Bibliography

Anon, Economic Times, 1991, July 18, August 23, December 7,10,11.

Ahluwalia, M.S., State-Level Performance under Economic Reforms in India, Chicago University, 2002.

Arvind Virmani, Growth and Poverty, Policy Implication for Lagging States, Economic and Political Weekly, January, 2008.

Aslan, Aza, Tactics in Economic War, Statesman, April 26, 2009.

Barker, Earnest, Principles of Social and Political Theory, Oxford University Press, 1954.

Bhattacharya, B.B., Fiscal Management: Issues and Policy Options, Seminar of the Indian Economic Trust, 1991.

Bidwai Praful, IMF Packages, Dubious Economics Bad Politics, Economic Times, July 12, 1991.

Brahmananda, P.R., Probable Economic and Social Effects of New Economic Policy Structure, 9th G L Mehta Lecture, IIT Bombay, 1994.

Birdball, N., Why Inequality Matters in a Globalizing World?, Wider Annual Lecture, 2005.

Bardhan, Pranab, Social Justice in Global Economy, Economic and Political Weekly, February 3 to 10, 2007.

Basu, Deepak, Warming the Earth, Statesman, April 6, 2010.

Bjorn Lamberg, Cars Bombs and Climate Gate, Economic Times, December 2010.

Bose, D.N., Earth and the World, Statesman, 21 February, 2010.

Chandra, P. and Shukla, P.R., Manufacturing Excellence and Global Competitiveness, Economic and Political Weekly 1994, Vol. XXIX, No. 9.

Dutta B. Firmly on Trodden Path, Economic and Political Weekly, July 12, 1991.

Dutta, B., No Grand Finale, Not So After All, Statesman, July

30, 1991.

Dholakia, R.H., Spatial Dimension of Acceleration of Economic Growth, Economic and Political Weekly, 1994, Vol. XXIX, No. 35.

Dilip M. Nonchine, The Decades of Structural Reform in India-A Balance Sheet, Arthvijnan, September-December, 2007.

Dogra, Bharat. Life Style and Ecology, Statesman, 7th July, 2008.

EPW Research Foundation, Social Indicators of Development-Inter-state Disparities, Economic and Political Weekly, Vol. XXIX, No. 21.

Eric Hobsbawn, The Age of Extremes, The Short 20th Century 1915, 5, London.

Goswami, Prith, Economics of Environment-A Study of Durgapur Industrial Region, Ph.D. Thesis, Viswabharati University, 2002.

Greennage, A.H.J., Historical Introduction to Fourth Edition of Postes Gai us.

Gupta, R.C., Great Political Thinkers, East and West, L.N. Agrawal, Agra, 1988.

Government of India, Union Budget for 1991-92, Report of the Economic Advisory Council of Export and Imports, New Delhi 1989.

Galbraith, John Kenneth, New Political Economy, Vol. II, 1997.

Hollis, Chenery, Redistribution with Growth, Oxford University Press, London, 1975.

Harris, John, Border Lands of Economics, Indian Journal of Labour Economics, Vol. 46, 2003.

Ian Bateman, Environmental and Economic Appraisal, Environmental Science and Management, 1995.

H. Edward Stead and Jean Gamer Stead, Strategic Management for a Small Planet, Business and Environment, 1999.

Huntigton, Samuelson P., The Clash of Civilizations and the

Remarking of World Order, Simon and Schuster, New York, 1996.

Jaylor, L., Economic Openness-Problems to the Century's End, World Institute of Development Economic Research, Helbsanki, 1968.

Jacques, Harsh Ell and Bran, Liberalization and Communist Manifesto, Economic and Political Weekly, January 2000.

Kothari, Ashok, Environment and NPT, Economic and Political Weekly, April 29, 1995.

Kohli Atul, Politics of Economic Growth in Independent India, 1980-2005, Economic and Political Weekly, April 1, 2006.

Lenin, The State of Revolution.

Myrdal, G., Asian Drama: An Inquiry into the Poverty of Nations, New York, Random House, 1968.

Mundle, Sudipto and Rao, M. Govind, Volume and Composition of Government Subsidies in India, 1987-88, Economic and Political Weekly, Vol. XXVI.

Michel, Chossudovsky, Seattle and Beyond: Disarming New World Order, Economic and Political Weekly, November 15, 2000.

Meher, R., A Socio-Political-Cultural Study: Industry vs. Environment-The Case Study of Rourkela, Environment and Economic Development, 1996.

Nayak, P.B., Some Key issues in India's Current Economic Crisis at Seminar on Fiscal Management in Indian Economy: Issues and Policy Options, Indian Economic Trust, New Delhi, 1991.

Nayar, Deepak, Economic Growth in Independent India, Economic and Political Weekly, April 2006.

Patnaik, S.M., Displacement, Rehabilitation and Social Change, Inter-India Publication, 1996.

Parikh Kirits, et. Al, Natural Resources Accounting-A Framenode for India, The Challenge of the Balance (ed.), Amit Agarwal, 1997.

Paranjape, H.K., New Industrial Policy-Capital Manifesto, Economic and Political Weekly, October 26, 1991.

Patnaik, Prabhat, The Economic Crises, Economic Times, July 3, 1991.

Prime, Eshag E., Fiscal and Monetary Policies and Problems in Developing Countries, Cambridge University Press, 1985.

Pant Manoj, WTO Negotiation-Identity Interests not Positions, Economic Times, 31 August, 2001.

Prasad, P.M., Environment Protection: Role of Regulatory System in India, Economic and Political Weekly, April 1, 2006.

Ramesh Diwas and Mark Lutz, Introduction to the Book: Essays in Gandhi's Economics, Gandhian Foundation, 1985.

Raman, G.K., Industrial Polity: Half-baked Measures, Economic Times, August 14, 1991, and Prevention: Need for Safety Mechanism, Economic Times, December 7, 1991.

Reserve Bank of India, Annual Report, 1986, 1991.

Ranadive, K.R., Income Distribution: The Unsolving Puzzle, Indian Economic, Jr. Conference Issue, 1989.

Radhakrishan, R., Agricultural Growth, Employment and Poverty: A Policy Perspective, Economic and Political Weekly, January 19, 2002.

Sen, Rajkumar, From Diamond to Platinum, IEA Presidential Address, Indian Economic Trust for Research and Development, 1992.

Sanwat, Mukul, Climate Policy Needs a Basic Shift, Economic Times, January 13, 2010.

Sen, Amartya, The Argumentative Indian, Penguin Books, 2005.

Sen, Amartya, Resources, Values and Development, Oxford University Press, Delhi, 1984.

Singh, Ghana Shyam (ed.), Structural Changes in India, Har-Anand Publications, New Delhi, 1991.

Singh, A.K., Patterns of Regional Development, Oxford University Press, 1984.

Stiglitz, Joseph E., Turn Left for Sustainable Growth,

Economic Times, August 18, 2008.

Sahoo, Amarendra, Essays on the Indian Economy: Competitive Pressure, Productivity and Performance, Centre Dissertation Series, Tilburg University, Netherlands, 2008.

Sahoo, Basudeb (ed.) Economic Development of Environment, APH Publication, New Delhi, 1996.

Sahu, Nirmal Chandra, Economics of Pollution-A Case Study of Angul-Talcher Industrial Region in Orissa, Upgradation Course, Environment Economics, 1999.

Soma, Banerjee, Why Should We Pay for Big Emitters? Economic Times, 30 November, 2009.

Swaminnathan, S. and Ankelesaria Aiyer, Carbon Cuts Penalty or Insurance? Economic Times, 9 December, 2009.

Vaidyanthan, A., Employment Situation: Some Envisaging Perspectives, Economic and Political Weekly, Vol. XXIX, No. 5, 1994.

Walsten, Scou, Spreading Prosperity, Economic Times, June 25, 2003.

William, Son J.G., Regional Disparity and the Process of Development, Economic Development and Cultural Change, 1965, Vol. 13, No. 4.

William, E. James, S. Naya and G.M. Mier, Asian Development, International Centre for Economic Growth University of Wisconsin Press, 1987.

Index

Index